Knitted Babes

Claire Garland

Knitted Babes

Five Dolls & their Wardrobes to Knit & Stitch

Claire Garland

INTERWEAVE PRESS
www.interweave.com

First published in Great Britain in 2005 by
Mitchell Beazley, an imprint of Octopus Publishing Group Ltd,
2–4 Heron Quays, London E14 4JP

Senior Executive Editor Anna Sanderson
Executive Art Editor Christine Keilty
Editor Karen Hemingway
Pattern Checker Marilyn Wilson
Photography, Illustration, and Design John Garland
Proofreader Clare Hacking
Indexer Sue Farr
Production Seyhan Esen

First edition for North America published in 2005 by Interweave Press, Inc.

All inquiries should be addressed to:
Interweave Press, Inc.
201 East Fourth St.
Loveland, CO 80537 USA
www.interweave.com

ISBN 1-59668-000-8

Set in Helvetica

Color origination by Chroma Graphics (Overseas) Pte Ltd, Singapore
Printed and bound in China by Toppan Printing Company Ltd

Library of Congress Cataloging-in-Publication Data

Garland, Claire.
  Knitted babes : five dolls & their wardrobes to knit & stitch / Claire Garland.
      p. cm.
  Includes bibliographical references and index.
  ISBN 1-59668-000-8 (alk. paper)
  1. Rag doll making. 2. Rag dolls. 3. Doll clothes—Patterns. 4. Knitting—
Patterns. I. Title.
  TT175.G36 2005
  745.592'21—dc22
                                    2005005927

10 9 8 7 6 5 4 3 2 1

Contents

Babes' World

This book contains an appealing collection of five knitted dolls with all the charm of cherished rag dolls. Each doll has a winning personality and her own collection of unique garments and accessories. Knit the dolls with fingering-weight yarn, then knit or sew everything they need from old clothing, leftover balls of yarn, and scraps of fabric. Everything, from the basic doll to her smallest accessory, is quick and easy to make.

The dolls are knitted in stockinette stitch, then stuffed and seamed. All of the accessories are either knitted or sewn. In addition to stockinette stitch, you'll need to work garter stitch, seed stitch, and ribbing for the knitted pieces. The sewn pieces require a minimum of sewing supplies and only the most basic sewing skills.

Equipment

For the knitted projects, you'll need fingering-weight yarn and sizes 2 (2.75 mm) and 3 (3.25 mm) knitting needles. You'll also need a safety pin for holding stitches that aren't in use; a blunt-tipped tapestry needle to sew the knitted pieces together (using the yarn from each project); and scissors for cutting the yarn and loose ends.

For the sewn projects, you'll need a basic sewing kit that includes pins, needles, sewing thread, and scissors; tissue or tracing paper for transferring templates and motifs; and, if desired, a sewing machine (although all of the projects are small enough to be sewn by hand).

Yarn & Fabric

The projects in this book use fingering-weight yarn, felt and other colorful fabrics, and all sorts of trimmings.

Before knitting any of the projects, check your gauge to make sure the pattern will knit up to the correct size. To check your gauge, cast on the number of stitches and knit the number of rows specified to make a 4" (10 cm) square. If your square measures 4" (10 cm), then your gauge is correct. If your square is bigger, your stitches are too loose, and you should change to smaller needles. If your square is smaller, your stitches are too tight and you should change to larger needles. Change needles and reknit the square until you have the correct gauge.

You will also need scraps of felt and dress fabric in a variety of colors and patterns, as well as buttons, beads, elastic, and all types of trimmings. Scour the attic and thrift shops for worn out clothing and fascinating embellishments that can be given new purpose in a babe's wardrobe.

Knitting Know-how

This section explains all the basic knitting techniques you'll need for any of the projects in this book. Whether you're a novice knitter or just need to refresh your memory, review the following abbreviations and techniques before you begin.

Some of the projects include charted color patterns. The charts for these projects are on pages 122–125.

Remember to stay relaxed and enjoy your creation.

ENGLISH-LANGUAGE TERMINOLOGY

USA	UK
Bind off	Cast off
Seed stitch	Moss stitch
Gauge	Tension
Stockinette stitch	Stocking stitch
Yarnover (yo)	yf, yo

STANDARD ABBREVIATIONS

alt	alternate
beg	beginning
cont	continue
dec	decrease
inc	increase
K	knit
K-wise	knitwise; e.g., as if to knit
K1f&b	increase 1 stitch by knitting into a stitch as usual, then knitting into the back loop of the same stitch
P	purl
patt	pattern
P1f&b	increase 1 stitch by purling into a stitch as usual, then purling into the back loop of the same stitch
rem	remaining
rep	repeat
skp	slip a stitch, knit a stitch, pass the slipped stitch over the knitted stitch
sl	slip
st(s)	stitch(es)
St st	stockinette stitch
tbl	through back loop
tog	together
yf	bring the yarn forward
yo	bring the yarn over the needle
*	indicates a repeated section, which is explained in the design; e.g., "Repeat from * to end"
(...)	indicates a repeated section; e.g., "(K2tog, yf, K1) twice" means you should repeat the instructions inside the parentheses twice

HOLDING THE NEEDLES AND YARN

There are various ways to hold yarn and needles for knitting. Below are the three most common methods. Try them all to see which technique is most comfortable for you.

English method

Place one hand on top of each needle and use your thumb, index, and middle fingers to hold the needles. Hold the yarn in your right hand by passing it under and around the little finger, over the ring finger, under the middle finger, and over the index finger. To make a stitch (*see* page 15), temporarily hold both needles with your left hand while you use your right index finger to wind the working yarn over the tip of the right needle, using your little finger to control the tension (the tightness/looseness) of the yarn.

Continental method

Hold one needle in each hand as explained for the English method, but in this case, hold the yarn in your left hand by wrapping it around your little finger, then over the top of your index finger. Use the right-hand needle to make the stitches as described on page 15, while controlling the tension with your left hand.

French method

Hold the left-hand needle from above, as described for the English method, but hold the right-hand needle from below, as if to hold a pencil. Tension the yarn with your right hand as for the English method and use your right index finger to guide the yarn as you make the stitches as described on page 15.

SLIPKNOT

Most knitting starts with a slipknot, which becomes the very first stitch on the needle.

1 Wind the working yarn around your left index finger from front to back, then around to the back again to form a circle. Slide the circle of yarn off your finger and push a loop of working yarn through the circle from back to front. Place the tip of a knitting needle under this loop, to pull it out from the circle (illustration 1).

2 Pull the loose tail of yarn down away from the needle to tighten the loop until it is snug (but not overly tight) on the needle (illustration 2). Pull on the working yarn (the end attached to the yarn ball) to loosen the knot.

CASTING ON

There are many methods to cast stitches onto the needle, any of which will work for the designs in this book. Feel free to use the method that feels most comfortable for you. If you are unsure of which method to use, use the knitted method shown here. This type of cast-on is suitable for all applications and produces a strong, neat edge.

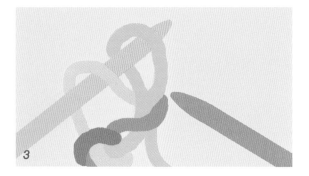

1 Leaving a tail about 6" (15 cm) long, make a slipknot and place it on the left-hand needle. Holding the yarn at the back of the left needle, insert the tip of the right-hand needle into the slipknot from the front to the back.

2 Pass the working yarn (the yarn that's attached to the ball) around the tip of the right needle so that it crosses the front of the needle (illustration 1).

3 With the left-hand needle still in the slipknot, draw the right-hand needle and the working yarn forwards through the slipknot to make a loop on the right-hand needle (illustration 2).

4 Place the newly formed loop onto the left-hand needle, twisting it as you do so (illustraton 3), and remove the right-hand needle. There are now two stitches on the left-hand needle.

To cast on more stitches, insert the right-hand needle into the front of the stitch just made (the one closest to the needle tip) and then repeat steps 1 to 4. Repeat this process until you have the required number of stitches on the left needle.

Now you're ready to knit or purl as described on page 15.

MAKING A KNIT STITCH

A knit stitch is usually worked on the right side of a piece.

1 With the cast-on stitches on the left-hand needle, insert the tip of the right-hand needle into the first stitch from the front to the back. Holding the yarn at the back of the needles, bring the working yarn around the tip of the right needle, so it is between the right and left needles (illustration 1).

2 Use the right-hand needle to draw the yarn forward through the stitch on the left-hand needle, thereby making a new stitch on the right-hand needle (illustration 2). Slip the original stitch off the left needle.

Repeat steps 1 and 2 for each knit stitch. Knit every stitch of every row to produce garter stitch.

MAKING A PURL STITCH

A purl stitch is usually worked on the wrong side of a piece.

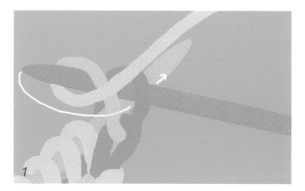

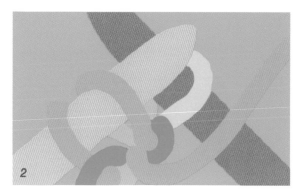

1 With the cast-on stitches on the left-hand needle, bring the working yarn to the front of the work. Insert the right-hand needle through the first stitch on the left needle from the back to the front, then wind the working yarn over the tip of the right needle from the right to the left (illustration 1).

2 Use the right-hand needle to draw the yarn through the stitch on the left-hand needle, thereby making a new stitch on the right-hand needle (illustration 2). Slip the original stitch off the left needle.

Repeat steps 1 and 2 for each purl stitch. Alternate a row of knit stitches with a row of purl stitches to produce stockinette stitch.

ADDING TEXTURE

You can get an array of interesting textures by combining knit and purl stitches. The two examples shown here are used in this book.

Ribbing

Ribbing is made by alternating columns of knit stitches and purl stitches. Ribbing makes a tidy edge that is often used for cuffs, waistbands, and button bands. Single rib alternates one knit stitch with one purl stitch; double rib alternates two knit stitches with two purl stitches.

To work single (K1, P1) rib:
Row 1: Take the yarn to the back of the work and knit one stitch, then bring the yarn to the front of the work and purl one stitch. Repeat these two stitches to the end of the row. The pattern might read: *K1, P1; repeat from * to end of row.
Row 2: Purl one stitch, then knit one stitch. Repeat these two stitches to the end of the row. The pattern might read: *P1, K1; repeat from * to end of row.

To work double (K2, P2) rib:
Row 1: *K2, P2; repeat from * to end of row.
Row 2: *P2, K2; repeat from * to end of row.

Seed stitch

Seed stitch also alternates knit and purl stitches and can substitute for ribbing. To work seed stitch, knit the first stitch then purl the second one. Repeat these two stitches to the end of the row, as for single rib. The second row is worked in the same way, alternating one knit stitch with one purl stitch, but the stitches are offset so that the knit stitches are worked on top of the purl stitches of the previous row and the purl stitches are woked on top of the knit stitches.

SHAPING

There are several ways to shape a knitted piece. The following three techniques are commonly used.

Short rows

Short rows are used to shape shoulder and neck edges. To work a short row, knit or purl as directed to where the pattern reads "turn." Then, even though there are still stitches on the left-hand needle, turn the work around as if you were at the end of the row, and work back across the stitches you just worked. Continue on that section of stitches as directed.

Increasing stitches

Increases are used to add width to a knitted piece. The simplest method is to work into the front and back loops of the same stitch to make two stitches from one.

1 Work to where the extra stitch is needed. Knit or purl through the front of the stitch as usual, but do not drop the stitch off the left-hand needle.

2 With the yarn at the back of the work, insert the tip of the right-hand needle into the back loop of the stitch still on the left-hand needle (shown in illustration above), and knit or purl that loop as if it were another stitch. Slip the original stitch off the left needle.

Decreasing stitches

Decreases are used to narrow the width of a knitted piece. To decrease, two stitches are worked together.

Knit two together (k2tog)

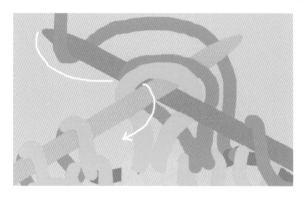

For a knit row, insert the tip of the right-hand needle from left to right into the second stitch, then into the first stitch on the left-hand needle, then knit the two stitches together as if they were a single stitch.

Purl two together (p2tog)

On a purl row, insert the right-hand needle from right to left through the first two stitches on the left-hand needle, then purl them together as if they were a single stitch.

BINDING OFF

At the end of a knitted piece, the stitches need to be bound off so that the knitting does not unravel.

1 Knit or purl the first two stitches according to the pattern, so that both stitches are on the right-hand needle.

2 Use the tip of the left-hand needle to lift the first stitch (shown as a white outline in the illustration above) up and over the second stitch, and then off the right-hand needle. Knit or purl the next stitch on the left needle. Repeat this step until one stitch remains on the right needle.

3 Pull the last stitch to lengthen it. Break the working yarn, leaving a long tail for sewing up the seam, if desired. Then thread the tail through the lengthened stitch, and pull on the tail to tighten and secure the last stitch.

PICKING UP STITCHES

For some projects, stitches are added to the edge of a knitted piece and worked in a different direction. To do this, use a needle to draw loops of yarn through the previously knitted stitches to create new stitches directly onto the needle.

Along a straight edge

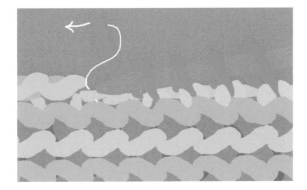

1 Start at the position specified in the instructions, holding the knitted piece in your left hand with the right side of the piece facing you. Insert the tip of the right-hand needle from front to back through the center of the first stitch at the edge of the knitted piece. Wind the yarn around the right-hand needle from back to front, as if to knit.

2 Draw the loop of yarn through the edge stitch to form a new stitch on the right-hand needle.

Continue to pick up a loop for each stitch along the edge of the knitted piece in this manner until you have the required number of stitches.

Along a curved or diagonal edge

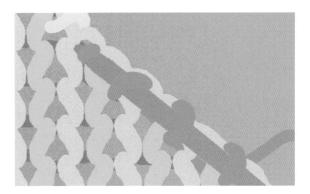

1 Start at the position specified in the instructions, holding the knitted piece in your left hand with the right side of the piece facing you. Insert the tip of the right-hand needle from front to back between the first and second stitches along the edge of the knitted piece. Wind the yarn around the right-hand needle from back to front, as if to knit.

2 Draw the loop of yarn through the knitting to form a new stitch on the right-hand needle.

Continue to pick up loops between stitches along the edge of the knitting in this manner until you have the required number of stitches.

SEAMING

There are a number of ways to join knitted pieces together. The two methods used in this book are worked with yarn threaded on a blunt-tipped tapestry needle.

Mattress stitch

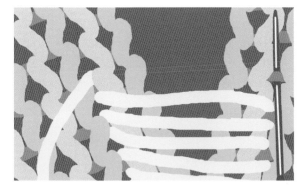

Also known as invisible seaming, the mattress stitch is widely used for joining side and sleeve seams. It produces a flat seam with little bulk.

1 Place the two pieces to be joined side by side, right sides up, matching stitch for stitch. Thread a tapestry needle with a length of matching yarn.

2 Bring the tapestry needle out through the center of the first stitch on one piece, just above the bind-off edge. Slip the needle through the center of the corresponding stitch on the other piece and out through the center of the stitch above it. Then insert the needle through the center of the first stitch on the first piece again and out through the center of the stitch above it. Continue in this way along the entire seam.

Backstitch

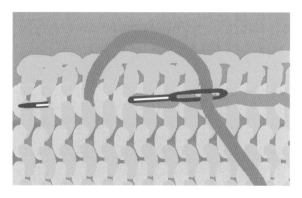

A backstitch is commonly used for shoulder seams, where a firm seam is required to hold the shape of the knitted pieces.

1 Pin the two pieces together with right sides facing each other, matching stitch for stitch. Thread a tapestry with a length of matching yarn. Working from right to left, bring the threaded needle to the front of the work, one stitch in from the edge of each piece. Take the needle from front to back around the cast-on/bind-off edge and back through to the front, two stitches to the left of the original stitch.

2 Take the needle down two stitches to the right, at the end of the previous stitch. Bring the needle up again two stitches to the left of where it previously came up. Repeat this step along the entire edge.

Sew or weave in loose ends by threading them onto a tapestry needle and working running stitches along the edge of the knitted piece. Sew through the bars between the stitches and work the yarn back on itself to secure the end.

COLOR PATTERNS

Some of the projects in this book involve color patterns. Three techniques can be used.

Stripes

To add a new color for a striped pattern, join the new yarn at the beginning of a row. Leaving long tails of both the new and old yarn (long enough to weave in later), simply knot the new yarn to the old one. Slip the knot close to the work, then knit or purl the first stitch as usual. When the knitting is complete, untie the knot and weave in the yarn tails or use them to sew up the seams.

Color stranding

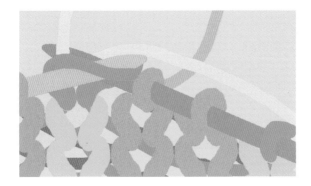

1 To work two or more colors in a single row according to a charted pattern you will need to strand the yarn across the back of the work. Work the first color for the specified number of stitches. When a new color is needed, drop the first color, leaving the yarn hanging at the back. Leaving a long tail hanging at the back, pick up the new color, and work it for the specified number of stitches.

2 To change back to a color used earlier in a row, drop the color no longer needed and pick up the new color, bringing it over the top of the old color, and continue with it for the sepcified number of stitches. Strand the yarn not in use loosely across the back of the work so that the work doesn't pucker.

Swiss darning or duplicate stitch

Swiss darning is a simple way to add a color pattern on top of finished stockinette stitch. Thread the desired color of yarn on a tapestry needle. Secure the yarn at the back of the work. Bring the threaded needle up through the middle of a knitted stitch. Follow the path of the yarn in the knitted piece, duplicating the stitch in the new color, until all of the desired stitches have been covered.

SPECIAL TECHNIQUES

All of the projects in this book are easy to knit. Just take the instructions one step at a time as you go. Only two special techniques are used. One is a special way to increase a stitch, the other is a special way to decrease a stitch. The two are often used in tandem to create holes (or eyelets) without changing the overall number of stitches in a row.

Yarnover (yo) increase

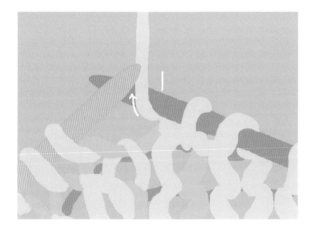

Work to the point where the instructions read "yo." If you are knitting, simply bring the yarn to the front between the needles then take it over the right-hand needle before knitting the next stitch. If you are purling, take the yarn over the right-hand needle then bring the yarn to the front between the needles. The yarn will form a simple loop over the needle that is not connected to a stitch in the previous row.

A yarnover increase is commonly used in conjunction with decrease to form a small hole or eyelet without changing the overall number of stitches, as for the eyelets in DD Diva's drawstring bag and the tiny buttonholes in Dot's Blue Bubbles Cardigan.

Slip, knit, pass (skp) decrease

The skp technique is usually worked on knit (right-side) rows. It is used for decreasing and shaping a knitted piece to give a fashioned detail, as in Rudy's Lacy Woolen Shawl.

1 Work to the point where the instructions read "skp." Slip the next stitch from the left-hand needle to the right-hand needle without knitting it. Knit the next stitch.

2 Insert the tip of the left-hand needle into the slipped stitch, then lift the slipped stitch over the knitted stitch and off the right-hand needle.

Sewing Know-how

All of the sewn items in this book take just minutes to make and require only the most basic sewing supplies. Instructions for the stitches and techniques are outlined on the following pages. Refer to the list of terms below when following the instructions for the projects.

TERMINOLOGY

Appliqué	fabric shape applied by hand or machine to a background fabric
Bias	45-degree angle to the selvedge; fabric is cut on the bias to make bindings and cover fabrics
Binding	narrow bias strip of fabric, either bought ready-made or handmade
Clipping	cutting into a seam allowance to ease the fabric around a curve or cutting across the corner of a seam allowance to reduce bulk
Dots	positional guides to be transferred from the pattern to the fabric
Fat quarter	A quarter-yard of fabric that measures 18" (45.5 cm) x 22" (56 cm)
Gathering stitch	a straight stitch, slightly longer than a running stitch, worked by hand or machine; the ends are not secured but drawn up to gather the fabric
Grainline	the straight grain of the fabric, either parallel to the selvedge or across the width of the fabric; it is indicated by a long arrow on a pattern that must be aligned with the widthwise or lengthwise grain of the fabric
Miter	a diagonal seam joining two pieces of fabric at a corner to reduce bulk along a hemmed edge
Pinking	cutting fabric with zigzag edges to prevent fraying
Pinking shears	zigzag-bladed scissors used for pinking edges
Fold line	indicates where the fabric should be folded; sometimes a fold line occurs on the edge of a pattern piece and must be aligned with a fold on the fabric before cutting out; i.e., the pattern shows only half of the complete shape
Quilting	two layers of fabrics sandwiching a layer of padding and stitched together
Seam allowance	extra fabric needed to make a seam
Selvedge	the finished, woven edge of fabric as manufactured
Zigzag stitch	a machine stitch used for binding edges on seams or appliqué, or for decoration

TRANSFERRING SEWING PATTERNS

The templates for the sewn garments and the motifs used as appliqués are provided on pages 110–121.

Photocopy the template or motif, enlarging it if necessary to the size specified to make the pattern pieces. Make note of the number of pieces you'll need to cut from each template. Pin the pattern pieces to the chosen fabric, taking care to align the grainline arrow with the straight grain of the fabric and, if necessary, placing any fold lines along a fold in the fabric. Cut out each shape along the solid outer line. Transfer any dots, notches, or other markings to the fabric.

MEASURING

You may choose to design your own clothes for the dolls. The easiest way to do this is to look at other clothes—turn them inside out to see how they were made and examine the shapes that make up an entire garment.

Replicate the same shapes on paper, scaling them down to suit your doll's measurements. The critical measurements you will want to follow are the circumferences of the chest, waist, and head, and the length of the arms and legs—the measurements shown on the photograph at right here are approximate; be sure to measure your own doll. Add a seam allowance of about ¼" (6 mm) around each pattern piece.

SEWING

To sew the pieces of a garment together, pin the pieces together as specified (usually right sides together). If desired, baste them together, removing the pins as you

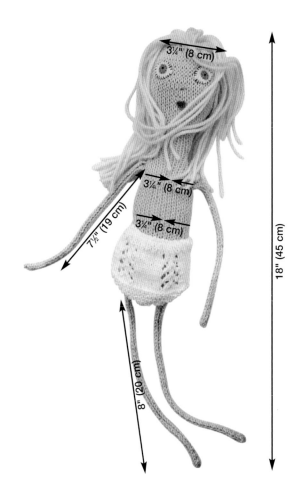

baste. Leaving the seam allowance specified by the pattern, use an average-sized stitch to hand- or machine sew along the seam line. Remove the pins and basting stitches, if there are any. Finish the raw edges of the seam allowance by sewing a machine zigzag stitch or by pinking them with pinking shears.

Press the seam open with a cool iron, unless the pattern directs otherwise.

SEWING STITCHES

You only need to know a few sewing stitches to complete any of the projects in this book.

Slip stitch

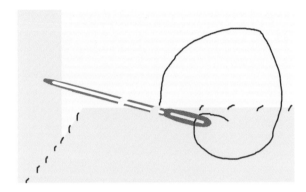

To sew a basic hem, thread a sewing needle with matching thread. Secure the thread to the fabric by making a small knot on the wrong side of the fabric.

Working from right to left, bring the threaded needle up through the single layer of fabric, make a nearly invisible stitch by picking up a few threads in the folded fabric of the hem, then bring the needle back through the single layer of fabric, then out again.

To add a pocket:
You can add a pocket detail on any of the doll's clothes, for example Bunny's Gala Gown. Try patch pockets on pants or add a fabric pocket to a knitted garment.

Cut a rectangle of fabric the desired size, making sure to add seam allowances. Turn under the side and bottom edges. Trim, miter, and slip-stitch the corners on the wrong side. Turn a double hem along the top edge, and miter the top corners as before.

Pin and baste the pocket to the garment, right side facing up and aligned with the straight grain of the garment fabric. Slip-stitch in place.

Running stitch

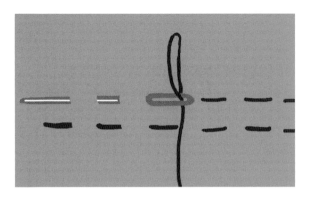

Running stitches are used to sew seams or to add decorative top stitches. Secure the thread on the wrong side of the fabric and take small, even stitches with even spaces. For added security, sew a second line of stitches parallel to the first.

A gathering stitch is worked in the same way but with longer stitches. Don't secure the thread at either end, but use it to gather up the fabric.

Basting stitch

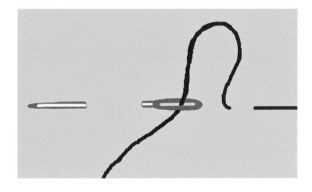

Basting stitches are temporary stitches that hold two pieces of fabric in place until they are stitched together permanently. Work basting stitches as long running stitches with equally long gaps between the stitches.

French knot

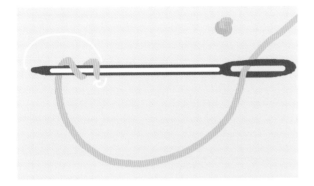

Sitting like a bead on top of the fabric, a French knot is both decorative and textural. Bring the threaded needle through to the front of the fabric. Wind the thread twice around the tip of the needle. Keeping the wraps taut, re-insert the needle close to where it first emerged. Pull the thread through, making sure the knot holds its shape. Secure the thread at the back.

Buttonhole stitch

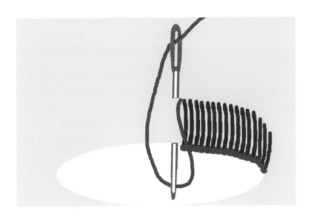

The buttonhole stitch is used to finish the raw edges of a buttonhole, as well as for decoration. Thread a needle with matching thread and secure it at one edge of the opening. Bring the threaded needle to the front at the raw edge. Insert the needle from front to back through the fabric a short distance from the raw edge, to emerge again at the raw edge from the back. Loop the working thread around the tip of the needle, and pull the needle through to tighten the thread snug around the edge of the fabric. Continue around the entire opening, making evenly spaced stitches. Finish by securing the thread at the back of the work.

If you don't want to bother with real buttonholes, you can create faux buttonholes by using snaps or velcro tape. Sew the buttons in position on the overlapping fabric. Then sew one half of the snap or velcro on the wrong side of the fabric, directly beneath each button. Sew the other half of the snap or velcro in the corresponding position on the other garment piece.

MAKING A CASING

Make a casing to hold elastic for the waistband of a skirt or pants, or a drawstring for a bag.

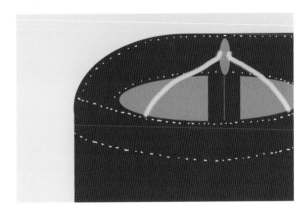

Fold the casing allowance to the wrong side, then fold under the raw edge. Use a running stitch to sew the casing in place along both folded edges, leaving an opening in the bottom line of stitching. Or, if the casing runs across a seam, carefully unpick the wrong side of the seam between the two rows of stitches. Thread the elastic or drawstring through the casing. Sew the ends of the elastic together securely, then slip the elastic inside the casing. Slip-stitch the casing closed.

How to Make the Babes

MATERIALS One 50-gram ball of fingering-weight yarn in skin color • Toy stuffing • Yarn for hair • Scraps of felt for eyes and mouth • Sewing thread for eyes, nose, and mouth details • Size 2 (2.75 mm) needles • Tapestry needle for attaching hair • Embroidery needle for adding facial features

GAUGE 30 sts x 38 rows = 4" (10 cm) in St st on size 2 (2.75 mm) needles

ABBREVIATIONS *See* page 12

INSTRUCTIONS

Body

Make two; one front and one back.

Cast on 18 sts.

Mark the 3rd and 16th sts to indicate the outside thigh position for each leg.

Beg with a K row, work 38 rows in St st.

Dec row: K2tog, K to last 2 sts, K2tog (16 sts).

Next row: P2tog, P to last 2 sts, P2tog (14 sts).

Mark each end of row to indicate underarm positions.

Cont to dec 1 st at each end of every row until there are 8 sts.

Shape head: Work 3 rows even in St st.

Inc row: Inc 1 st at each end of row (10 sts).

Next row: P.

Rep the last 2 rows until there are 28 sts.

Work 15 rows even in St st.

Dec row: K2tog all across the row (14 sts).

Next row: P.

Dec row: K2tog all across the row (7 sts).

Bind off.

FINISHING

Sew the body back to the front with right sides facing, leaving an opening at the lower edge for turning.

Turn right side out. Lightly stuff the body. Sew the opening closed.

Arms

Make two.

Cast on 4 sts.

Work in St st until piece measures 8" (20 cm).

Bind off.

Weave in the loose ends. Sew the bind-on edge of each arm to the body at the underarm markers. The side edges of the arms will curl in naturally; there is no need to join them with a seam.

Legs

Make two.

Cast on 6 sts.

Work in St st until piece measures 9½" (24 cm). (For longer "spaghetti" legs as shown on page 89, work the legs 1" longer.)

Bind off.

Weave in the loose ends. Sew the cast-on edge of each leg to the marked outside thigh position on the body. Just like the arms, the sides of the legs will curl in naturally.

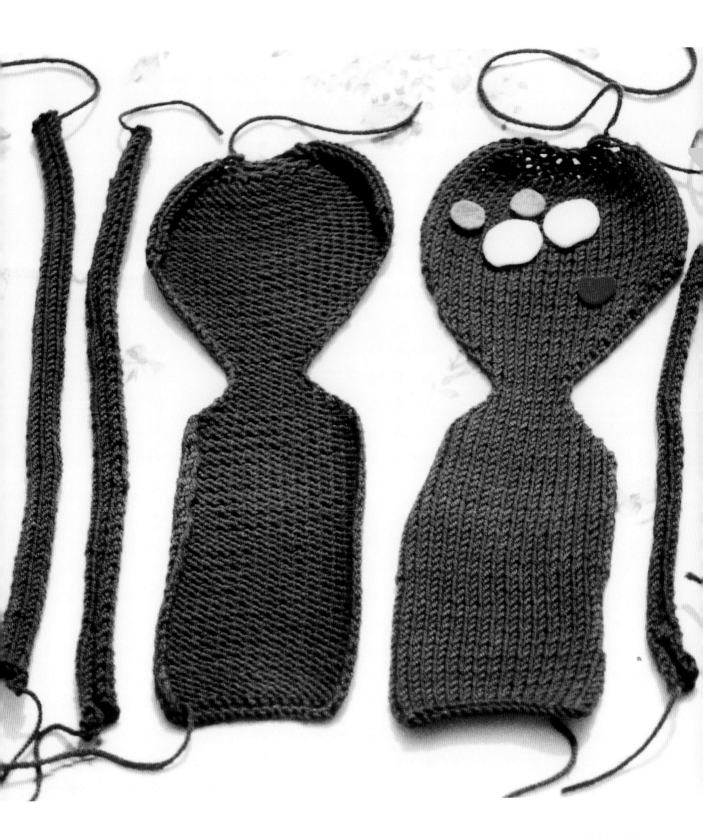

Creating the Look

Because there are so many ways to vary the details and give character, your babe can have a look as individual as your own. The best place to start is with the facial features.

Templates

The basic templates for the eyes and lips are given on page 114. Use them at the size provided, or enlarge or reduce them on a photocopier to suit your doll. Using the templates as a guide, cut the eyes (make sure they're the same size) and lips out of felt.

Eyes

Pin the eye whites and irises in a pleasing arrangement on the doll's face. Experiment with the position—close together, far apart, even at a gentle slant. A good guideline is to place the outer edges of the eyes at least five stitches in from the sides of the head and nine stitches down from the crown.

Sew the iris to the white with a double strand of black thread to create a "pupil." Secure the thread at the back of the white, bring the needle through the center of both the white and the iris, then make a French knot or a few straight stitches to make the pupil. Or, cut out small circles of black felt for the pupils and glue the pieces together with fabric glue.

Sew straight stitches radiating around the iris onto the white in a color to match or contrast with the iris.

Attach the eyes to the doll's face with black thread, working straight stitches that radiate around the white to imitate eyelashes.

Lips

Pin the felt lips to the doll's face. With matching (or slightly contrasting) thread and a sewing needle, sew tiny stitches to sew them in place, extending the stitches beyond the felt if desired. Vary the placement and the color of the stitches to give your doll different pouts and smiles.

Finishing touches

Add a cute nose with the same thread used to sew the lips in place—simply sew a few straight stitches across one or two of the knitted stitches between the lips and the eyes.

Finally, create freckles or beauty spots by adding a light dusting of French knots.

Completing the Look

Once you have designed your babe's face, it's time to add the hair. You may already know just how you want to style her hair. If not, here are a few ideas.

You and your child can have hours of fun choosing just the right yarn for the doll's hair—there are so many options. Use mohair yarn to create a full head of fluffy fairy hair. Use kinky yarn raveled from a piece of knitting to make marvelous curls. Or make larger curls by twisting yarn around your finger to form coils, then slipping the coils off your finger and gently steaming them to "set" the curls.

Whatever the look and style you choose, prepare the hair as a single unit before attaching it to the doll's head. First, cut strands of yarn slightly longer than double the desired length—you can always trim them later. Group the strands into bundles, and with matching thread and a sewing needle, securely sew the centers of the bundles together. Add bundles until you have the look you want.

Place the hair on the doll's head with the centers of the bundles aligned at the top of the head. Using matching thread and a sewing needle, attach the hair securely to the head, working from front to back.

Style the hair by cutting the yarn into cheeky layers or a sleek bob. Tie the yarn into a ponytail, pigtails, or braids. Twist the yarn and fasten it to the doll's head in a sophisticated chignon.

Add ribbons, scrunchies, felt flowers, or a headband. Thread beads onto the ends of single strands or groups of yarn. Change the look at your will—you can be a perpetual hairdresser!

SAFETY NOTE

Do not use small buttons or beads, or fluffy yarns on dolls for children under three years of age. Use washable stuffing that conforms to safety standards, sew seams and attach trimming securely, and be sure to remove all pins and needles before giving the doll to a child.

Dot Pebbles

This petite, totally cool, sun-sand-and-surf chick is a regular water babe. Dot is vivacious and breezy, and always on the go. She spends her days on the beach, catching rays when the sun shines—and it shines all the time, of course! Dot's clothes reflect her free, summer lifestyle—relaxed yet fitted for active play. They're totally cool, a little bit retro, and as easy as the proverbial pie. So-oo today! Everyone loves gorgeous little Dot.

Beach Gear

Sleeveless Seersucker Blouse • Board Cords and Sand Slides • Blue Bubbles Cardigan • Lifesaver Bather • Dot 4 T-shirt • Retro Beachbag • Floral Swim Hat • Go Speedy Swimsuit Set • Rubber Duck Ring • Striped Slip-on Dress

Sleeveless Seersucker Blouse

A cool breezy blouse with miniature buttons

MATERIALS Fat quarter of seersucker fabric • 2 tiny buttons • 2 snaps • Basic sewing kit

NOTE All seams are ¼" (6 mm) wide and stitched with right sides facing, unless stated otherwise.

INSTRUCTIONS

1 Photocopy or transfer the template on page 118 at 100 percent. Fold the fabric in half and pin the pattern pieces to the fabric as detailed on page 23. Cut out the pieces as directed and transfer the pattern markings to the fabric.

2 Fold the opening edges of both front pieces to the wrong side, along the fold lines. Turn under ⅛" (3 mm) along both raw edges for hems. Press, then sew both hems in place.

3 Sew fronts to back along the shoulder seams. Press.

4 Pin one collar to one collar stand, right sides facing, matching the dots and the long edges between the dots. Sew the seam and press open. Repeat for the other collar.

5 Pin the two collars together with right sides facing. Seam them from the neck edge of the collar stand, around the three straight edges of the collar, and to the other neck edge. Trim the corners and turn the collar right side out. Press.

6 Press under ¼" (6 mm) along the neck edge of both collar stands. Slip-stitch the right side of one collar stand to the wrong side of the blouse neck. Top-stitch the edge of the other collar stand while attaching it to the right side of the neck edge and concealing the raw edges. Top-stitch collar ⅛" (3 mm) from the outer edges. Press.

7 Make two vertical buttonholes, spacing them evenly down the right front. Work a buttonhole stitch around the buttonholes to reinforce. Sew two buttons onto the left front opposite the buttonholes (for more detail, *see* page 25).

8 Turn under a double ⅛" (3 mm) hem around the armholes and sew in place.

9 Turn under a double ⅛" (3 mm) hem around the bottom edge of the blouse and sew in place. Press.

For Dot's bandanna, cut a piece of coordinating fabric measuring 12" (30 cm) square. Sew a running stitch all around the square, ¼" (6 mm) from the edges. Fray the edges up to the stitching.

Fold the bandanna in half diagonally and tie it at the back of Dot's head.

Board Cords and Sand Slides

Hipster cords with a polka-dot skirt team up with slick sandles

MATERIALS Worn-out corduroy fabric or fat quarter of baby cord • 11 x 2" (28 x 5 cm) retro-patterned fabric for the skirt • Scrap of felt for star motif • ¼" (6 mm) -wide elastic • Basic sewing kit • Safety pin

NOTE All seams are ¼" (6 mm) wide and stitched with right sides facing, unless stated otherwise.

INSTRUCTIONS

1 Fray one long edge of the skirt panel to make a ¼" (6 mm) fringe.

2 Enlarge the pants template on page 111 to 167 percent. Fold the pants fabric and pin the pattern pieces to the fabric as detailed on page 23. Cut out the pieces.

3 Press under a ¼" (6 mm) facing along the long unfrayed edge of the skirt. Sew the side seam. Turn the skirt right side out.

4 Sew each pants front to the matching pants back, along the outside and inside leg seams.

5 Turn one leg right side out and slip it inside the other leg, right sides facing. Matching the waist edges and inside leg seams, sew the legs together along the center front and back seams. Turn right side out.

6 Fold a ⅜" (10 mm) facing to the right side around the waist edge of the pants. Match the wrong side of the skirt to the right side of the pants, aligning the top edges. Sew around the top edge, close to the folds. Sew another row of stitches ¼" (6 mm) down from the first, leaving an opening for elastic. Cut elastic to fit the waist and, using a safety pin, thread it through the casing. Join the ends securely and sew the opening closed.

7 Using the template on page 121, cut a star motif out of felt. Attach it with running stitches near the bottom edge of one leg of the pants. Fray the bottom edges of the legs. Press.

MATERIALS FOR SLIDES Fingering-weight yarn • Size 2 (2.75 mm) needles • Tapestry needle

INSTRUCTIONS

Make two.

For the sole, cast on 14 sts. Work 22 rows in garter st. Bind off. Fold the strip into thirds widthwise and sew together.

For the strap, cast on 3 sts in a contrasting color. Work 14 rows in garter st. Bind off. Sew the ends of each strap to the opposite sides of each sole.

Blue Bubbles Cardigan

A contrasting edging and bubble details in a casual cardigan

MATERIALS Fingering-weight yarn in blue (M), brown, pink, and white • Size 2 (2.75 mm) needles • Two ⅜" (1 cm) buttons • Safety pin • Tapestry needle

GAUGE 30 sts x 38 rows = 4" (10 cm) in St st on size 2 (2.75 mm) needles

ABBREVIATIONS *See page 12*

NOTE Use a photocopier to enlarge the chart on page 124 for ease of reading. Read chart from right to left on odd-numbered (K) rows and from left to right on even (P) rows, stranding the yarn not in use across the back of the work.

INSTRUCTIONS

Back

Using B, cast on 31 sts. Work in single rib as follows:

Row 1: K1, *P1, K1; rep from * to end.
Row 2: P1, *K1, P1; rep from * to end.
Rep the last 2 rows once more.
Change to M. Beg with a K row, work in St st for 14 rows.
Shape armholes: Bind off 2 sts at beg of the next 2 rows (27 sts).
Next row: K3, K2tog, K to last 5 sts, K2tog, K3 (25 sts).
Next row: P.

Rep the last 2 rows until there are 21 sts. Work 7 rows even in St st.
Shape shoulders: Bind off 5 sts at beg of next 2 rows. Place rem 11 sts on a safety pin.

Left front

Using B, cast on 16 sts. Work 4 rows in single rib as follows:
*K1, P1; rep from * to end.
Change to M and work St st for 8 rows**.
Work even in St st for 6 more rows.
Shape armholes: Bind off 2 sts, K to end (14 sts).
Next row: P.
Next row: K3, K2tog, K to end (13 sts).
Rep the last 2 rows once more (12 sts).
Next row: P.
Shape neck: ***K3, K2tog, K to last 5 sts, K2tog, K3 (10 sts).
Next row: P3, P2tog, P to end (9 sts).
Next row: K to last 5 sts, K2tog, K3 (8 sts).
Rep the last 2 rows until 5 sts rem.
Work 2 rows St st, end at armhole edge.
Bind off.

Right front

Work as for left front to**.
Next row: K7, change to W and K2.
Change to M and K to end.

Cont to follow patt from chart on page 124, taking note of shapings as follows:

Shape armhole: Bind off 2 sts, P to end.

Next row: K to last 5 sts, K2tog, K3 (13 sts).

Next row: P.

Cont to dec in this manner until there are 12 sts, ending with a P row.

Shape neck: Work as for left front from *** to end, reversing shapings (dec at end of P rows and beg of K rows).

Sleeves

Make two; work charted bubble pattern on just one.

Using B, cast on 29 sts. Work 4 rows in single rib as for back.

Change to M. Beg with K row, work even in St st for 33 rows.

Shaping: Bind off 2 sts at beg of next 2 rows (25 sts).

Next row: P3, P2tog, P to last 5 sts, P2tog, P3 (23 sts).

Next row: K.

Rep the last 2 rows twice more (19 sts).

Next row: P3, P2tog, purl to last 5 sts, P2tog, P3 (17 sts).

Bind off 3 sts at beg of every row until 5 sts rem. Bind off rem sts.

Sew shoulder seams.

Buttonhole band

With right side of piece facing, pick up and K: 27 sts up right front edge, 11 sts from safety pin, and 27 sts down left front edge (65 sts). Work single rib for 1 row.

Next row: Work two buttonholes as follows: Rib 4, *yo, P2tog, rib 8; rep from * once more, rib to end.

Work 1 row single rib. Bind off.

Sew buttons opposite buttonholes.

FINISHING

Weave in loose ends. Lightly steam the pieces to block. Sew the side and sleeve seams. Sew the sleeves into the armholes.

Lifesaver Bather

This fun piece is a cross between a wet suit and a one-piece swimsuit.

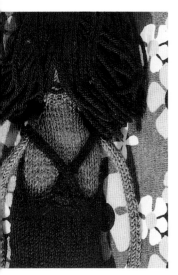

MATERIALS Fingering-weight yarn in red (M), white, and blue • Size 2 (2.75 mm) needles • Safety pin • Tapestry needle

GAUGE 30 sts x 38 rows = 4" (10 cm) in St st on size 2 (2.75 mm) needles

ABBREVIATIONS *See* page 12

NOTE Use a photocopier to enlarge the chart on page 123. Read chart from right to left on odd-numbered (K) rows and from left to right on even (P) rows, stranding the yarn not in use across the back of the work.

INSTRUCTIONS

Front

Front right leg: Using M, cast on 13 sts. Work single rib as follows:

**Row 1: K1, *P1, K1; rep from * to end.

Row 2: P1, *K1, P1; rep from * to end.

Rep the last 2 rows once more.

Next row: Beg with K row, work St st for 8 rows**.

Cast on 2 sts (15 sts). Break yarn. Place sts on a safety pin.

Front left leg: Cast on 13 sts and work as for right leg from ** to **.

Next row: K13, K15 on safety pin (28 sts). Work St st for 9 rows***.

Pattern: Continue in St st, work the charted patt over the next 22 rows.

Shape armholes: Dec 1 st at each end of this K row (26 sts).

Next row: P.

Next row: K2tog, K to last 2 sts, K2tog (24 sts).

Next row: P.

Next row: K.

Next row: P2tog, P to last 2 sts, P2tog (22 sts).

Next row: K.

Rep last 2 rows twice more (18 sts).

Next row: P2tog, P to last 2 sts, P2tog (16 sts).

Shoulder straps: K2tog, K3, turn and work these 4 sts in St st for 26 rows for left strap. Bind off. Rejoin yarn at inside edge, bind off 6 sts, K to last 2 sts, K2tog (4 sts). Continue as for left strap.

Back

Work as for front right leg and front left leg to ***. Cont even in St st for 15 rows.

Shape back: P8, turn and work on these sts only.

Next row: (K2tog) twice, K to end (6 sts).

Next row: P.

Rep the last 2 rows twice more (2 sts).

Bind off these 2 sts.

Rejoin yarn to rem 20 sts.

Bind off 12 sts, P to end (8 sts).

Next row: K to last 4 sts, (K2tog) twice (6 sts).

Next row: P.

Rep last 2 rows twice more (2 sts).

Bind off.

FINISHING

Weave in loose ends. Gently steam the knitting flat. Sew the side and inside leg seams. Cross the straps at the back and attach the bind-off ends to the waist edge, 1" (2.5 cm) in from the side seams.

This suit is open to many variations. Work it without the charted pattern, or substitute colorful stripes, or alternate rows of garter stitch and stockinette stitch for textural bands. Experiment with different colors and textures, and add a few surprises along the way!

Extra Babe Things

Make a snappy little shirt from scraps of worn-out T-shirts that are patched together.

Cut scraps of knitted T-shirts to make two 5" (12.5 cm) squares (for the front and back), and two 2½" (6 cm) squares (for the sleeves). Using the templates on page 119 at 100 percent, cut out the garment pieces. Fold each sleeve in half lengthwise with right sides together. Sew a ⅛" (3 mm) seam along the long edge. Turn under and sew a small hem at the cuff. Turn right side out.

With right sides together, join the front and back at the shoulders with a ¼" (6 mm) seam. Turn under and sew a ¼" (6 mm) hem around the front and back neckline. With right sides together, sew the sides together with a ¼" (6 mm) seam, leaving openings for the sleeves. Turn right side out. Insert the sleeves into the armhole openings and sew in place. Hem the bottom edge. Embroider the doll's name onto a separate scrap of fabric and sew it to the shirt front.

Take time to choose just the right fabrics, buttons, and trimmings to match your doll's personality. Just as you and your child have individual styles, so do the dolls that you make.

Personalizing garments, such as the "Dot 4" T-shirt, and making fun accessories like the Rubber Duck Ring, help to give each doll her individual personality.

Recycle tiny buttons from old doll and baby clothes. Sort through containers of old buttons or beads at thrift shops and rummage sales—they were once carefully chosen for garments that are now past their prime. They deserve to be given a new lease on life.

Make this tiny bag in minutes using fabric scraps. Add a square of different fabric for a simple detail.

To make the bag, cut a piece of fabric to measure 9½ x 4¾" (24 x 12 cm). Press ¼" (6 mm) to the wrong side along one long edge. Fold over another 2" (5 cm) to make a drawstring casing and sew in place. At each end of the casing, turn under and sew a ¼" (6 mm) hem.

Fold the fabric in half lengthways, right sides together, and press. Open it out and sew a square scrap of contrasting fabric, frayed around the edges, on the bag front.

Fold the bag fabric in half again and sew along the side and bottom edges. Turn the bag right side out and thread a length of cord through the drawstring casing.

To make a bathing towel, simply knit a 4" (10 cm) square of fingering yarn in garter stitch. Add fringe to opposite ends of the square.

Accessories can be easy to design and quick to make. This swim hat is adapted from a standard knitted hat.

To make the swim hat, knit the crown as for the hat on page 55. To make a strap, cast on 20 sts. Knit 2 rows. Bind off. Repeat for the second strap. Attach one end of each strap to opposite sides of the hat.

Cut out 15 felt flowers, following the flower motif on page 121 at 100 percent. Attach the flowers securely to the hat by sewing one stitch in the center of each flower.

Go Speedy Swimsuit Set

This swimsuit has go-fast stripes and a matching duck ring

MATERIALS FOR SWIMSUIT Small amounts of fingering-weight yarn in lilac (L), yellow (Y), and turquoise (T) • Size 2 (2.75 mm) needles • Tapestry needle

GAUGE 28 sts x 48 rows = 4" (10 cm) in garter st on size 2 (2.75 mm) needles

ABBREVIATIONS *See page 12*

INSTRUCTIONS

Work the back and front the same.
Start at the gusset with L, cast on 6 sts.
K 1 row.
Inc row: K1, K1f&b, K to last 2 sts, K1f&b, K1 (8 sts).
Rep the inc row until there are 26 sts.
Change to Y, K 2 rows. Change back to L, K 2 rows. Change back to Y, K 14 rows.
Next row: Change to T, and K.
Next row: P.
Work St st for 6 rows, ending with a P row.
Shoulder straps: Bind off 3 sts. K3 inlcuding stitch used to bind off (3 sts).
Turn and work St st for 22 rows. Bind off.
Rejoin yarn. Bind off 14 sts, K to end (6 sts). Bind off 3 sts, P to end (3 sts). Cont in St st as for first strap. Bind off.

FINISHING

Join the cast-on edges at the gusset.
Sew the side and shoulder seams.

MATERIALS FOR DUCK RING Small amounts of fingering-weight yarn in yellow (Y) and beige (B) • Size 2 (2.75 mm) needles • Small piece of yellow felt • Black thread • Toy stuffing

GAUGE 28 sts x 48 rows = 4" (10 cm) in garter st on size 2 (2.75 mm) needles

INSTRUCTIONS

Ring: Cast on 20 sts in Y. Work garter st until piece measures 11" (28 cm). Bind off.
Duck's head: (make 2) Starting at the bill end with B, cast on 8 sts.
Next row: K1f&b in every st (16 sts).
Beg with a P row, work St st for 11 rows.
Next row: (K2tog) 3 times, K1f&b in next 4 sts, (K2tog) 3 times (14 sts).
P 1 row. Work St st for 5 rows. Bind off.

FINISHING

Fold the ring in half lengthways and sew the long seam. Firmly stuff the ring and sew the two ends together.

Sew the two head pieces together, leaving an opening for stuffing. Stuff the head, then sew the remaining seam. Following the template on page 113, cut two bills from felt. Sew the bills to the cast-on edges of the head. With black thread, make French knots for the eyes. Sew the head to the ring.

Striped Slip-on Dress

Easy wear doesn't come much easier than this casual cap-sleeved sundress. Chill out!

MATERIALS Fingering-weight cotton yarn in turquoise (T) and gold (G)
• Size 3 (3.25 mm) needles • Tapestry needle

GAUGE 23 sts x 32 rows = 4" (10 cm) in garter st on size 3 (3.25 mm) needles

ABBREVIATIONS *See* page 12

INSTRUCTIONS

(Knit in one piece.) Using T, cast on 70 sts. Work 2 rows in garter st.

Rows 3 and 4: Change to G and rep the last 2 rows.

Rows 5–26: Rep the last 4 rows to form striped patt for 22 more rows.

Row 27: K.

Dec row: K2, *K2tog; rep from * to last 2 sts, K2 (37 sts).

Next row: K.

Dec row: K1, *K2tog; rep from * to end (19 sts).

Knit 9 rows even in stripe patt.

Shape back waist: Bind off 2 sts, K to last 2 sts, bind off 2 sts (15 sts).

Rejoin yarn to center of rem 15 sts.

K 10 rows in stripe patt.

Left strap: K4, bind off 7 sts, K to end. Cont on last 4 sts, K 12 rows.

Next row: Dec 1 st at each end of needle (2 sts).

K 2 rows. Bind off.

Rejoin yarn to rem 4 sts at neck edge and work right strap to match left strap.

FINISHING

Sew the back seam. Sew the bind-off ends of the straps to the waist edge of the dress back.

Try different color combinations for other striking effects. There's no need to limit yourself to just two colors. Go for psychedelic vibrancy, clash or contrast colors. Give Dot a different dress for every day of the week!

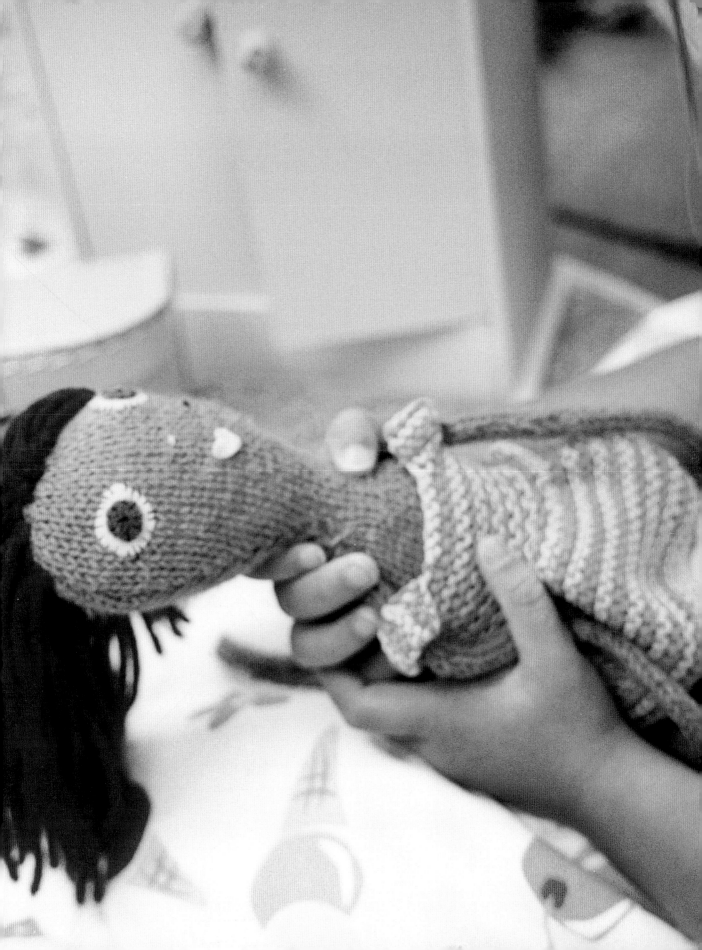

Bunny Bright

An ethereal, sweet-natured beauty, Bunny Bright has a sweet tooth and a penchant for ice-cream sodas. She's a café-bar star—cappuccinos, sodas, and sorbets are her lifestyle. Bunny has a voracious appetite for glamorous movie-star gowns and gossip. But however fluffy and floaty her style may be, Bunny always remains a devoted friend.

Frock Shop
Gingham Gala Gown with Glamour Hat • Pink Knit Bag • Butterfly Mules • Sparkly Ribbon-tied Gown • Flower Power Mini • Funky Psychedelic A-line • Lacy Undies • Sequin Bag • Flip-flops • 50s-style Bag • Two-tone Mules • Yellow Mules • Dolly Bag • Retro Pink Floral Polo Top

Gingham Gala Gown with Glamour Hat

This elegant gown comes with cross-stitch detail, a felted flower corsage, and a special-occasion hat

MATERIALS FOR GOWN

⅓ yd (30 cm) gingham fabric • Hooks and eyes • Scraps of felt • Basic sewing kit • Embroidery thread (optional)

NOTE All seams are ¼" (6 mm) wide and stitched with right sides facing, unless stated otherwise.

INSTRUCTIONS

1 Begin by making the bodice. Cut a strip of gingham measuring 4 x 3¼" (10 x 8 cm). Fold the strip in half lengthways, aligning the edges. Sew a seam along each short end. Press the seams open. Turn the band right side out. Press. Sew hooks and eyes, equally spaced, on the two short edges that form the bodice back.

2 Cut a strip of gingham measuring 8 x 2" (20 x 5 cm) for the shawl and make it in the same manner as the bodice, but without the hooks and eyes.

3 To make the skirt, cut a piece of gingham to measure 12 x 10" (30 x 25 cm). Sew a seam to join the two short ends. Press the seam open.

4 Run a gathering stitch around the waist edge and draw up the thread until the skirt width matches the bottom of the bodice.

5 Sew the gathered waist to the bodice, matching the back seam to the back edges of the bodice.

6 Turn and sew a double ¼" (6 mm) hem around the bottom edge of the skirt.

7 Cut the felt corsage following the flower motif on page 121. Sew it in place.

8 Sew a pocket to the skirt, following the instructions on page 24. Add embroidery if you wish, using the photograph as a guide.

9 Use a few discreet stitches to attach the shawl to the back of the bodice. When the dress is on the doll, sweep the shawl over both shoulders and secure with a loose knot at the back.

Change the look of the dress by adding small sleeves from narrow bands of gingham or straps of rickrack or ribbon. Before attaching the sleeves permanently, adjust them for the best position while the dress is on the doll.

MATERIALS FOR HAT

Fingering-weight yarn • Size 2 (2.75 mm)
needles • Tapestry needle

INSTRUCTIONS

Crown

Cast on 17 sts. K 5 rows.

Next row: Dec 1 st at each end of row
(15 sts).

Rep the last 6 rows once more (13 sts).
K 3 rows.

Next row: Dec 1 st at each end of row
(11 sts).

Rep the last 4 rows until 5 sts rem.

Next row: Dec 1 st at each end of
row (3 sts). Bind off.

Make 3 more pieces to match.

Join the four pieces leaving the
cast-on edges open.

Brim

Cast on 7 sts. K 2 rows.

Next 2 rows: K5, turn, K back.

Rep the last 4 rows until the shorter edge
of the brim fits along the cast-on edges of
the crown. Bind off.

FINISHING

Join ends neatly then sew the brim to the
hat. Add felt flowers.

Extra Babe Things

This pink bag is knitted in one piece in garter stitch, and lined with contrasting fabric.

Cast on 20 sts. Working in garter st, K 1 row. Then inc 1 st into the first and last st on the next and every 6th row, until there are 28 sts on the needle. Bind off.

Fold the bag in half lengthways across the cast-on and bind-off edges, and sew the selvedge edges together to form a bag shape. Position the seam so it is centered at the back of the bag, then sew the base together along the cast-on edge. Turn the bag inside out.

Make a lining of similar dimensions from contrasting fabric. Turn under the top edge, slip the lining over the knitted bag, wrong sides facing, and handsew in place. Turn the bag right sides out.

Make a twisted cord out of two 6" (15 cm) lengths of yarn. Knot the ends and sew one end to each side of the bag.

Let your child join in the fun by helping to make the doll's accessories.

Children love to thread beads and are quite capable at very young ages. Threading beads helps children to develop hand-eye coordination and—when they know that they are helping you—gives them a satisfying sense of achievement.

Tie a bead onto one end of a length of fine elastic and set your child free with the bead tin to create a unique string of pearls, plastic gems, or sparkly faux jewels. You'll both find real pleasure in these shared, quiet moments!

No gown is complete without a butterfly slipper. Even a knitted one can be fit for a princess.

Gauge Using fingering-weight yarn, 30 sts x 38 rows = 4" (10 cm) in St st on size 2 (2.75 mm) needles

Slipper sole: Cast on 8 sts. Work 14 rows in St st. Bind off.

Slipper upper: Beg at the toe end, cast on 3 sts.

Row 1: K.

Next row: K, inc in every st (6 sts).

Rep the last 2 rows once (12 sts). K 5 rows. Bind off.

To make up: Press the sole flat and fold it lengthways with purl sides facing. Stitch the edges together. Position the seam under the sole and sew the cast-on edges together at the slipper toe, and the bind-off edges together at the slipper heel. Shape the slipper upper over the tip of your index finger, then lay it over the toe end of the sole, and sew in place. Following the motif on page 120, cut out a felt butterfly and sew it to the slipper upper.

Satin ribbons add a touch of luxury to Bunny's, or any of the other babe's, wardrobe.

Have fun adding outrageous beads, buttons, trimmings, and bows. These dolls, and the children they are made for, love elaborate glittery and ribbony accessories.

However, do be careful to attach small buttons and embellishments very securely so that they stay in place. Due to the possibility of choking, do not use very small trimmings for dolls that will be used by children under three years of age.

Sparkly Ribbon-tied Gown and Flower Power Mini

This 50s-style satin and florals sundress has a fitted bodice

MATERIALS **For both**: Fabric for upper bodice, lining, and skirt • Ribbons • Braid • Basic sewing kit
For the mini: Bias binding for the armhole trim • Two buttons

NOTE All seams are ¼" (6 mm) wide and stitched with right sides facing, unless stated otherwise.

LONG GOWN INSTRUCTIONS

1 Enlarge the bodice front template on page 110 to 143 percent. Cut one for the bodice and one for the lining.

2 Cut four 4" (10 cm) ribbons. Pin two ribbons to each shoulder.

3 Sew the lining to the bodice front along the neck, shoulders (securing the ribbons), and side seams. Trim the corners and turn right side out. Press.

4 To make the skirt, cut a fabric rectangle measuring 12 x 10" (30 x 25 cm). Fold it widthwise, align the short edges, and sew the back seam. Press the seam.

5 Run a gathering stitch around the waist edge and draw up the thread until the waist is twice the bodice width. Sew the bodice to the gathered waist edge,

aligning the back seam to the back of the dress. Fold and sew a double ¼" (6 mm) hem along the bottom edge. Trim the waist with ribbons or braid.

MINI INSTRUCTIONS

1 Enlarge the bodice templates on page 110 to 143 percent. Cut out two bodice and two lining pieces. Sew the two bodice pieces together at shoulders and side. Repeat for the lining. Sew lining to bodice around the neckline. Clip the curves and turn right side out. Press.

2 For the skirt, cut a piece of the fabric to measure 6 x 9" (15 x 23 cm). Gather the waist edge to fit the bodice. Complete the skirt as for the long gown.

3 Attach bias binding around the armholes, right sides facing, beginning and ending at the side seams. Slip-stitch the free edge of the binding to the lining side of the bodice.

4 Turn in and sew the open back edges. Make two buttonholes on the right back. Sew buttons to the left back, opposite the buttonholes. Sew braid or ribbon around the waist, leaving a length to tie at the back.

Funky Psychedelic A-Line

A really retro revival raver to wear over lacy undies

MATERIALS FOR DRESS Fat quarter of 70s-style fabric • Matching fabric for lining • Basic sewing kit

NOTE All seams are ¼" (6 mm) wide and stitched with right sides facing, unless stated otherwise.

INSTRUCTIONS

1 Enlarge the templates on pages 116–117 to 143 percent. Cut two dress pieces from the main fabric and two bodice pieces from the lining fabric.

2 Sew the lining to the bodice fronts and backs around the neck, back opening, and armholes. Clip into the curves and turn right sides out. Press.

3 Sew together the shoulder and side seams of the main dress. Press seams open. Fold under the same seams on the lining and slip-stitch in place. Press.

4 Turn and sew a double ⅛" (3 mm) hem around the bottom edge of the dress.

To make a headband, cut a piece of the dress fabric to measure 6 x 1½" (15 x 4 cm). Fold it in half lengthwise, right sides facing. Sew around the edges, leaving an opening for turning. Trim the corners and turn right sides out. Press. Sew the opening closed.

MATERIALS FOR UNDIES

Fingering-weight cotton yarn in white • Size 2 (2.75 mm) needles • 8" (20 cm) shirring elastic

GAUGE 30 sts x 38 rows = 4" (10 cm) in garter st on size 2 (2.75 mm) needles

ABBREVIATIONS *See* page 12

INSTRUCTIONS

Work the back and front alike. Beg at the gusset, cast on 6 sts. K 2 rows.

Next row: K1, yo, K to last st, yo, K1 (8 sts). Rep this row until there are 28 sts. Work patt as follows:

Row 1: K5, yo, K2tog, K1, K2tog, yo, K8, yo, K2tog, K1, K2tog, yo, K to end.

Row 2: P.

Row 3: K6, yo, sl1, K2tog, psso, yo, K10, yo, sl1, K2tog, psso, yo, K to end.

Row 4: P.

Cont in patt until piece measures 2½" (6.5 cm) from cast-on edge.

Rib: *K1, P1; rep from * to end.

Rep the last row 3 times more. Bind off.

FINISHING

Sew the gusset and side seams. Thread shirring elastic through the rib at the waist.

Essential Accessories

All of the accessories in this section can be made within a couple of hours. Make several to complement the wardrobe of any of the babes.

Note All the templates are on pages 114–115. All seams are ¼" (6 mm) wide and stitched with right sides facing, unless stated otherwise.

Sequin bag

Cut one strap and one bag shape from felt. Fold the bag shape as directed, wrong sides facing, and sew the sides close to the edges. Sew each end of the strap to the top of the bag sides. Cut a buttonhole in the flap and sew a bead on the main bag to act as a button. Sew sequins over the front of the bag and along the strap.

Flip-flops

Cut four flip-flop shapes from felt. Sew two together with even running stitches close to the edges. Cut a toe strap and sew it in place on the sole as shown on the template. Repeat for the other flip-flop. Letting your imagination run wild, add colorful decorations.

50s-style bag

Cut out the bag shapes from fabric and felt as directed. Fold the fabric in half and sew up the edges with a ¹⁄₁₆" (2 mm) seam. Push in the corners and hold to finger press. Hem the short edges. Attach each end of the strap to the top of the bag, also securing the top corners of the bag. Slip-stitch the flap along the top back edge. Cut a buttonhole in the flap, sew a bead on the bag, and button it up.

Two-tone mules with knitted straps

To make the straps, use size 2 (2.75 mm) needles and fingering-weight yarn. Cast on 10 sts. Work 2 rows in K1, P1 rib. Bind off. Make another strap to match.

Cut out four sole shapes, two from pink felt and two from white. Sew a pink and a white shape together with a running stitch, securing each end of a strap on opposite sides of the sole. Repeat for the other mule.

Yellow mules

For the soles, use size 2 (2.75 mm) needles and fingering-weight yarn. Cast on 14 sts. Work 14 rows in St st. Cut the yarn. Remove the sts from the needle and thread the yarn tail through the sts, gather them up, and tie off the yarn to shape the toe. Fold the knitting in thirds across the cast-on edge and sew up the edges.

For the mule uppers, cast on 2 sts. Beg with a K row, work in St st and inc 1 st at each end of this row, then every alternate row, until there are 12 sts. Bind off.

Attach an upper to the sole of each mule, matching the center of the cast-on edge of the upper with the toe end of the sole.

Drawstring dolly bag

Cut a rectangle of fabric measuring 6 x 3" (15 x 7.5 cm). Fold the fabric in half widthwise. Sew a seam down each side of the bag, starting 1" (2.5 cm) from the top edge. Press the seams and open edges flat. Sew running stitches along the open side edges.

Turn under ¼" (6 mm), then ¾" (2 cm) along both top edges to make a drawstring casing. Sew casing in place. Turn the bag right side out. Thread braid or twisted yarn through the casing. Tie to secure the ends.

Retro Pink Floral Polo Top

An exuberant woolen top for a country garden party

MATERIALS Fingering-weight yarn in brown (B), cream (C), and raspberry pink (R) • Size 2 (2.75 mm) needles • Three safety pins • Tapestry needle • Six snaps

GAUGE 30 sts x 38 rows = 4" (10 cm) in St st on size 2 (2.75 mm) needles

ABBREVIATIONS See page 12

NOTE Use a photocopier to enlarge the chart on page 124 for ease of reading. Read chart from right to left on odd-numbered (K) rows and from left to right on even (P) rows, stranding the yarn not in use across the back of the work.

INSTRUCTIONS

Using R, cast on 60 sts.

Row 1: *K1, P1; rep from * to end.

Rep the last row 5 more times.

Change to colors B and C.

Next row: Following the patt on the chart and beg on a K row, cont in St st for 26 rows, ending with a P row.

Shape armholes: K11, turn and work on these 11 sts in St st for 13 more rows, ending with a K row.

Shape shoulder: Bind off 4 sts, P to end (7 sts). Break yarn and slip sts onto a safety pin. With right side facing, rejoin yarn to rem sts. Bind off 8 sts for armhole, K until there are 22 sts on right needle. Turn. Cont on these 22 sts for 4 more rows, ending with a P row.

Next row: K4, turn and work these 4 sts in St st for 9 more rows. Bind off.

Return to next 18 sts. Slip the first 14 sts onto another safety pin. Rejoin yarn, K4, turn. Work these 4 sts in St st for 9 more rows. Bind off.

Return to rem 19 sts. Rejoin yarn, bind off first 8 sts for armhole, K to end. Work rem 11 sts in St st for 15 rows, ending with a P row.

Shape shoulder: Bind off 4 sts, K to end. Break yarn and slip sts onto a safety pin.

With right sides facing, join shoulder and side seams.

Neckband: With right side facing, rejoin R. K across 7 sts on left back from last safety pin; pick up and K8 sts down to sts on safety pin; K14 sts from second safety pin; pick up and K8 sts up right front; K7 sts on right back from safety pin (44 sts). Work K1, P1 rib for 8 rows. Bind off in rib.

FINISHING

Sew six snaps at equal intervals along the back opening.

DD Diva

Elegant and wealthy, DD Diva is a princess who has it all—beauty, charisma, style, and a delightful sense of humor. And to top it off, she's also an Olympic diving champion! Her wardrobe, aptly named DD's Desirable Deco, reflects her flamboyant character. Carefree DD likes to travel to exotic and paradisical places, where she can practice her dives during the day and her dance moves late into the night.

DD's Desirable Deco
Flamenco Frill Top, Floral Hat, and Bell-bottom Pants • Denim Bell-bottoms, Calypso Sarong, and Chic Beret • Go Paradise Travel Bag • Two-tone Mules •Chunky Drawstring Bag • Rainbow Ribbons Twosome • Hoody and Swimsuit Set

Flamenco Frill Top, Floral Hat, and Bell-bottom Pants

DD loves these eclectic, colorful coordinates

MATERIALS Self-striping, or scraps of different colors (knit in random stripes throughout), of fingering-weight yarn • Size 2 (2.75 mm) needles • Scraps of felt for flower motifs • Tapestry needle
For the bell-bottoms: Small piece of baby corduroy • Basic sewing kit

GAUGE 30 sts x 38 rows = 4" (10 cm) in garter st on size 2 (2.75 mm) needles

ABBREVIATIONS *See page 12*

HAT INSTRUCTIONS
Crown
Cast on 17 sts. K 5 rows.

Next row: Dec 1 st at each end of row (15 sts).

Rep the last 6 rows once more.

K 3 rows.

Next row: Dec 1 st at each end of needle (13 sts).

Rep the last 4 rows until 5 sts rem.

Next row: Dec 1 st at each end of needle (11 sts).

Bind off. Make three more pieces to match. Sew the curved edges of the pieces together, leaving the cast-on edges open.

Brim
Cast on 7 sts. K 2 rows.

Next 2 rows: K5, turn, K back.

Rep the last 4 rows until shorter edge of brim fits around cast-on edges of crown. Bind off.

FINISHING
Join the short ends of brim to form a ring. Sew brim to hat. Using the motif on page 121, cut flowers out of felt. Sew to hat.

FRILL TOP INSTRUCTIONS
Starting with the back, cast on 100 sts.

Work in k1, p1 rib for 6 rows. K 10 rows.

Dec row: K2tog all across (50 sts).

K 8 rows.

Dec row: K2tog all across (25 sts)*.

Bind off. Work front as back to *.

Front straps: Bind off 2 sts, K4 including st used to bind off, turn and work these 4 sts in St st for 30 rows. Bind off.

Rejoin yarn, bind off 13 sts, K to end.

Next row: Bind off 2 sts, K to end (4 sts). Work rem 4 sts to match first strap.

FINISHING
Sew side seams. Tie straps around the back of the neck.

FLAMENCO FLARES
INSTRUCTIONS

Make the pants as the denim bell-bottoms
on page 72. Make two identical flared frills
as follows:

Cast on 30 sts. Work St st for 20 rows.

Next row: K2tog all across (15 sts).

Bind off.

FINISHING

Stitch one frill to the bottom hem
of each leg.

If you can't find self-striping yarn, simply
knit your own colorway of random stripes
of different colors of fingering-weight. *See*
page 20 for instructions on adding colors.

Denim Bell-bottoms, Calypso Sarong, and Chic Beret

These spangly sequin-detailed flares, baby-cord beret, and stylish sarong are set to jet set

MATERIALS Fine-weave fabric for sarong • Scrap of denim for bell-bottoms • Fabric remnant for frills • Short length of ¼" (6 mm) elastic • Small scrap of baby corduroy for beret • One button • Lace or braid trim • Basic sewing kit

NOTE All seams are ¼" (6 mm) and stitched with right sides facing, unless stated otherwise.

BELL-BOTTOMS INSTRUCTIONS

1 Enlarge the templates on page 111 to 167 percent. Cut out two back and two front pieces from the denim.

2 Align the outside and inside leg seams of each pair of back and front pieces. Sew the seams.

3 Turn one pant leg right side out. Pull the other leg over it, right sides facing, and sew the gusset seam.

4 Make a ⅜" (1 cm) casing all around the waist edge, leaving an opening for the elastic. Thread the elastic through the casing, tie or sew it to secure, and oversew the opening to close. Sew sequins to the waist edge.

5 For the frills, cut two pieces of fabric, each measuring 9 x 3" (23 x 7.5 cm). Make a ¼" (6 mm) hem along one long edge. Sew a gathering stitch along the opposite edge. Draw up the thread until the edge measures the same as the pant hemmed edge. Sew frill to the pant, with right sides facing.

SARONG INSTRUCTIONS

Cut a 6" (15 cm) square of fabric. Stitch a ¼" (6 mm) double hem around the edges.

BERET INSTRUCTIONS

1 Enlarge the template on page 115 to 143 percent. Cut six pieces from corduroy. Sew the six pieces together, side by side.

2 Sew a button to the center point. Attach lace or crocheted braid around the brim, leaving a long end to tie at the back.

Extra Babe Things

This little travel bag, ideal for jet-setting adventures, is made from scraps of felt and an old zipper.

From felt, cut two rectangles measuring 4¼ x 3¼" (11 x 8 cm) and one strip measuring 15 x 1½" (38 x 4 cm). Also cut four corner pieces, two handles, a small rectangle for the label, and an airplane motif following the motifs on page 121. Cut an old zipper to a length of 4" (10 cm).

Using the photograph as a guide, embroider "paradise" on the label, then use a running stitch to attach it, two corner pieces, and the airplane to one of the felt rectangles for the bag front. Sew the other corner pieces to the other rectangle for the bag back.

Cut a 4" (10 cm) slit in felt strip, centered both lengthwise and widthwise. Sew the zipper into the slit.

Sew the strip around all four edges of the bag front and bag back, with the zipper centered at the bag top, and securing the two handles as you go.

These diminutive two-tone yellow mules make a darling addition to DD's wardrobe.

Make two the same, using two shades of fingering-weight yarn and size 2 (2.75 mm) needles.

To make the soles, cast on 14 sts with the lighter color. Work in St st for 13 rows. Next row: P2tog all across (7 sts). Next row: K2tog, K to last 2 sts, K2tog (5 sts). Break the yarn, thread the tail through rem 5 sts, and gather them up. Fold lengthwise in thirds and sew in place.

To make the mule uppers, cast on 2 sts with the darker color. Beg with a K row, work in St st. Inc 1 st at each end of this and every other row until there are 10 sts. Next row: K4, K2tog, K4 (9 sts). Bind off. Sew the upper to the sole along the side edges, matching the cast-on edge of the upper to the toe end of the sole.

Made with sport-weight yarn, this chunky drawstring bag has a picot edge and bobble accent.
Using size 3 (3.25 mm) needles, cast on 26 sts. Work in garter st for 40 rows, changing colors as desired to make stripes. Work eyelets on the next row as follows: K1, *K2tog, yo, K1; rep from * to last st, K1. Work in garter st for 2 rows. Work the picot bind-off as follows: Bind off 1 st, *bind off 6 sts, transfer the st on the right needle to the left needle, cast on 3 sts; rep from * to end. Finish off. Sew the back seam. Twist or braid lengths of cotton yarn to make the drawstring. To work the bobble: Cast on 5 sts, work garter st for 5 rows, slip the second, third, fourth, and fifth sts over the top of the first st and off the needle. Cut the yarn, leaving a long tail. Use the tail to sew running stitches around the outer edge of the bobble, pull up the tail to gather the bobble, and sew it to the center of the drawstring. Thread the drawstring through the eyelets and tie the ends.

Use colorful sequins to add sparkly glamour to any of DD's sewn or knitted clothes.
You can turn a pair of wide-legged jeans into disco-fever flares by sewing a row of sequins around the waistband to make a spangled belt. Use matching or contrasting thread to sew the sequins wherever you want to add a splash of sparkle. Go wild and completely cover a sewn or knitted top with sequins to give DD a ravishingly decadent get-up.

If you'd prefer, you can work sequins directly into a knitted item. Just thread the sequins onto the knitting yarn—allow one sequin for each stitch you want to cover—before you begin to knit. Slide the sequins out of the way for the cast-on row, then as you knit, slide one sequin up to the needle with each stitch you want to cover, positioning the sequins flat against the right side of the work.

Rainbow Ribbons Twosome

This zippy little top-and-shorts number in jaunty, beachy stripes makes perfect deck gear

MATERIALS Old children's leggings or skirt with an elastic waistband • (or other colorful jersey fabric) • Basic sewing kit • ¼" (6 mm) elastic

NOTE All seams are ¼" (6 mm) and stitched with right sides facing, unless stated otherwise.

TOP INSTRUCTIONS

1 Cut a rectangle measuring 9 x 3" (23 x 7.5 cm) from the waistband area of the leggings or skirt. Include the elastic of the waistband, and pin the ends of the elastic, if necessary, to secure it.

2 Match the two short edges and sew the back seam.

3 Hem the non-elastic edge by machine with a zigzag or by hand with a blanket stitch.

4 To make the straps, cut two strips of the same fabric measuring 2 x ⅝" (5 x 1.5 cm). Fold in half lengthwise and sew around the edges, leaving an opening for turning.

5 Turn right side out and sew up the opening. Adjust the length of the straps on the doll and attach the ends to the elastic edge of the bodice.

PANTS INSTRUCTIONS

1 Enlarge the template on page 111 to 167 percent. Cut out two of each piece.

2 Align the outside and inside leg seams of each pair of back and front pieces. Sew the seams.

3 Turn one leg right side out. Pull the other leg over it, right sides facing, and sew the gusset seam.

4 Make a ⅜" (1 cm) casing around the waist edge, leaving an opening for the elastic (see page 25 for details). Thread the elastic through the casing, tie or sew it to secure, and sew the opening closed.

If you don't have suitably worn-out clothes to cut up, make this twosome out of any colorful jersey or cotton fabric. For the top, you will also need an 8" (20 cm) length of ⅜" (1 cm) wide elastic. Cut out two 4" (10 cm) squares of fabric. Sew the side seams. Turn under ½" (1.3 cm) for a casing. Sew the casing in place, then insert and secure the elastic. Hem the top and attach the shoulder straps.

Give DD a baseball cap by adding a felt brim to the beret template on page 115.

Hoody and Swimsuit Set

A personalized warm separate to wear over a sleek swimsuit

MATERIALS FOR HOODY

Fingering-weight yarn in blue (B) and off-white (W) • Size 2 (2.75 mm) needles • Tapestry needle

GAUGE
30 sts x 38 rows = 4" (10 cm) in St st on size 2 (2.75 mm) needles

ABBREVIATIONS *See page 12*

INSTRUCTIONS

Back

Using W, cast on 38 sts.

Work 2 rows in single rib as follows:

Row 1: K2, *P2, K2; rep from * to end.

Row 2: P2 *K2, P2; rep from * to end.

Stripe detail: Change to B and work 2 more rows in rib. Change back to W and work 2 more rows in rib.

Change to B and, beg with a K row, work 30 rows in St st. Mark each end of the last row to denote base of armholes.

Next row: Inc 1 st at each end of row (40 sts).

Work St st for 5 more rows.**

Rep the last 6 rows until there are 46 sts, ending with an inc row. Work 3 rows even in St st.

Divide for neck: K14, turn and work on 14 sts for the right shoulder.

Right shoulder: P2tog, P to end (13 sts).

Next row: Bind off 6 sts, K to last 2 sts, K2tog (6 sts).

Next row: P.

Bind off.

Left shoulder: Rejoin yarn to right side of rem sts. Bind off 18 sts, K to end (14 sts).

Next row: P to last 2 sts, P2tog (13 sts).

Next row: K2tog, K to end.

Next row: Bind off 6 sts, P to end (6 sts).

Next row: K.

Bind off.

Front

Work as for back to **, while at the same time incorporating the "D" pattern from the chart on page 125.

Divide for front opening: K1f&b, K18 (20 sts).

Turn and work these 20 sts for left front.

Left front: Work in St st for 5 rows.

Next row: K1f&b, K to end (21 sts).

Work in St st for 5 rows.

Next row: K1f&b, K to end (22 sts).

(**Note:** When you work the right front as directed on page 80, you will add a purl row here.)

Shape neck: Bind off 6 sts, P to end (16 sts).

Next row: K to last 2 sts, K2tog (15 sts).

Next row: P2tog, P to end.

Rep last 2 rows once more (12 sts).

Shape shoulder: Bind off 6 sts, K to end (6 sts).

Next row: P.
Bind off.

Right front: With RS facing, rejoin yarn to inner edge of rem 21 sts. Bind off 2 sts, K to last 2 sts, K1f&b, K1 (20 sts). Continue as for left front, but reverse shaping (increase for front opening at end of right-side rows and decrease for neck at beginning of right-side rows), and add a P row as noted. Sew shoulder seams.

Sleeves

Make two. With right sides facing and using B, pick up and K38 sts evenly spaced between the armhole markers. Beg with a P row, work in St st for 45 rows.
Work the ribbed cuffs as follows:
Row 1: K2, *P2, K2; rep from * to end.
Row 2: Change to W. P2, *K2, P2; rep from * to end.
Work 6 more rows in the ribbed stripe pattern as for the back. Bind off.

Hood

With right sides facing, rejoin B to right front neck, and pick up and K50 sts around the neck edge.
Next row: P.
Next row: K7, (K1, K1f&b, K2) 10 times, K3 (60 sts).
Work even in St st for 37 rows.
Shape hood back: K28, (K2tog) twice, K28 (58 sts).
Next row: P.

Next row: K27, (K2tog) twice, K27 (56 sts).
Next row: P.
Cont to dec as for the last two rows, working 1 st fewer on successive rows until 48 sts rem. Bind off.

FINISHING

Sew side and sleeve seams. Fold bind-off edge of hood in half and sew center seam.

MATERIALS FOR SWIMSUIT

Fingering-weight yarn in turquoise • Size 2 (2.75 mm) needles • Tapestry needle

GAUGE 28 sts x 38 rows = 4" (10 cm) in garter st on size 2 (2.75 mm) needles

ABBREVIATIONS *See page 12*

INSTRUCTIONS

Back

Starting at the gusset, cast on 6 sts.
K 1 row.
Inc row: K1f&b, K to last 2 sts, K1f&b, K1 (8 sts).
Rep the last row until there are 26 sts.
Work 30 rows even in garter st*.
Bind off.

Front

Work as for back to *.
Next row: P.
Next row: K2tog, K to last 2 sts, K2tog (24 sts).
Rep the last 2 rows until there are 18 sts.
P 1 row.

Right shoulder strap: K6, turn and work these sts as follows:

P2tog, P2, P2tog (4 sts).

**Next row: K4.

Next row: K1, P2, K1.

Rep the last 2 rows until strap measures 3" (7.5 cm). Bind off.

Left shoulder strap: Rejoin yarn to rem 12 sts.

Bind off 6 sts, K to end (6 sts).

Next row: P2tog, p2, p2tog (4 sts).

Work as for right shoulder strap from **. Bind off.

FINISHING

Sew gusset and side seams. Cross the straps at the back and sew to the upper back edge, 1" (2.5 cm) in from the side seams.

If desired, add bobble ties to the hoody. Twist or braid two lengths of yarn to make the ties, then make two bobbles as for the drawstring bag on page 75. Sew one bobble to each of each tie, and sew the other end of each tie to opposite sides of the hoody neck opening.

Complete the ensemble with a comfy blanket for DD to sit on. Make a rectangle measuring 6 x 3" (15 x 7.5 cm) in St st, following the charted "D" pattern if you wish. Add a contrasting border by knitting a ¾" (2 cm) strip of garter st long enough to wrap around the four edges of the rectangle. Weave in loose ends. Slip-stitch the garter border to the rectangle.

Flo Tilly

Delicate dancer Flo Tilly is a shinning star. Flo pirouettes her way through life in her own inimitable style—whether dressed up in a tutu to perform her *jeté* with cloud-like grace, or dressed down in sweats to relax and practice her moves with fellow dancers and friends. She works with precision and polish at her *pas glissé* and *pas de chat*. Flo's endless endurance ensures that she's the star of the show everywhere she goes.

Ballet Basics Fair Isle Pullover • Knitted Net Tutu • Pink Wrap-around Top • Slinky Sweat Band • Floaty Bias Ballet Skirt • Ballet Slippers • Simple Stripy Sweats • Floral Ballet Case

Fair Isle Pullover

This comfy sweater is just right to warm up and cool down

MATERIALS FOR SWEATER

Fingering-weight cotton in mauve (M), red, white, and black • Size 2 (2.75 mm) needles • Tapestry needle

GAUGE
30 sts x 38 rows = 4" (10 cm) in St st on size 2 (2.75 mm) needles

ABBREVIATIONS
See page 12

NOTE
Read the chart on page 122 from right to left on odd-numbered (K) rows, and from left to right on even (P) rows, stranding the yarn not in use across the back of the work.

INSTRUCTIONS

Work back and front alike. Using M, cast on 35 sts. Work single rib as follows:
Row 1: K1, *P1, K1; rep from * to end.
Row 2: P1, *K1, P1; rep from * to end.
Rep the last 2 rows once more.
Beg with a K row, work 3 rows in St st.
Chart: Work chart Rows 8 to 13.
Cont even in St st for 13 rows.
Shape armholes: Bind off 2 sts at beg of next 2 rows (31 sts).
Next row: K1, sl1, K1, psso, K to last 3 sts, K2tog, K1 (29 sts).
Next row: P.
Rep the last 2 rows until there are 15 sts.

Shape neck: Work 4 rows in single rib as follows:
Row 1: P1, *K1, P1; rep from * to end.
Row 2: K1, *P1, K1; rep from * to end.
Rep the last 2 rows once more. Bind off.

Sleeves

Make two. Using M, cast on 25 sts. Work single rib as follows:
Row 1: K1, *P1, K1; rep from * to end.
Row 2: P1, *K1, P1; rep from * to end.
Rep the last 2 rows once more.
Inc row: K1f&b, K to last 2 sts, K1f&b (27 sts).
Next row: P.
Rep inc row once (29 sts).
Cont even in St st for 3 rows, ending with a P row.
Rep the last 4 rows once more (31 sts).
Beg with a K row, cont in St st for 26 rows.
Shape raglan: Bind off 2 sts at beg of next 2 rows (27 sts).
Next row: K1, sl1, K1, psso, K to last 3 sts, K2tog, K1 (25 sts).
Next row: P.
Rep the last 2 rows until there are 11 sts.
Next row: K1, *P1, K1; rep from * to end.
Next row: P1, *K1, P1; rep from * to end.
Rep the last 2 rows once more.
Bind off.

FINISHING

Using a mattress stitch (*see* page 19), sew the sleeves to the front and back along the raglan edges. Sew the side and sleeve seams.

Don't be afraid to design your own Fair Isle pattern. It's easy to chart out a pattern on graph paper using colored pencils. Then knit, changing colors to match the colors on the chart as you go. From a simple patterned stripe to an allover pattern, you can design any sweater you'd like!

Knitted Net Tutu

This frothy, net confection is made for *pirouette* perfection

MATERIALS Fingering-weight cotton in pink • 20 x 10" (50 x 25 cm) netting in pink • Size 3 (3.25 mm) needles • Basic sewing kit • Tapestry needle

GAUGE 23 stitches x 32 rows = 4" (10 cm) in St st on size 3 (3.25 mm) needles

ABBREVIATIONS *See page 12*

INSTRUCTIONS

Tutu pants

Make two. Beginning at the bottom edge of the tutu, cast on 6 sts.

Row 1: P.

Inc row: K1f&b, K to last 2 sts, K1f&b, K1 (8 sts).

Rep last 2 rows until there are 16 sts. Work 3 rows even.* Bind off.

Tutu back

Cast on 6 sts. Work as for pants to * (16 sts). Cont in St st for 28 rows.**

Armhole: Work K2tog at each end of next 2 K rows (12 sts).

Next row: P.

Next row: K6, turn.

Right strap: P2tog, P to end (5 sts).

Next row: K to last 2 sts, k2tog (4 sts).

Work 4 rows in St st. Bind off.

Left strap: Rejoin yarn to rem 6 sts, K2tog, K to end (5 sts).

Next row: P to last 2 sts, P2tog (4 sts). Work 4 rows in St st. Bind off.

Tutu front

Work as tutu back to **.

Shoulder straps: K3 and turn. Work these 3 sts in St st for 8 rows. Bind off.

Rejoin yarn and bind off 10 sts (3 sts). Work rem 3 sts in St st for 8 rows. Bind off.

FINISHING

Sew the pants gusset and side seams, and the tutu shoulder and side seams.

Fold the net in half lengthwise and sew together with a ¼" (6 mm) allowance.

Sew a gathering stitch around the folded waist edge of the net. Gather the thread so that the net fits around the bottom edge of the tutu, and sew in place. Sew the pants to the body under the net. Trim net if desired.

To make the skirt separately, fold the net in half lengthwise and stitch a ⅜" (1 cm) casing along the folded edge. Sew the back seam to the casing. Thread elastic through the casing and pull it to fit the doll's waist. Tie or sew the ends of the elastic to secure, and stitch the casing opening closed.

Pink Wrap-around Top

A cozy wrap top for relaxing moments

MATERIALS Fingering-weight cotton yarn in pink • Size 3 (3.25 mm) needles • Tapestry needle

GAUGE 23 sts x 32 rows = 4" (10 cm) in St st on size 3 (3.25 mm) needles

ABBREVIATIONS *See* page 12

INSTRUCTIONS

Work from the lower back, over the shoulders, and down the fronts one piece.
Beg at the lower back, cast on 28 sts.
Beg with a K row, work St st for 24 rows, marking each end of the 9th row for base of armholes.

Shape neck: K9, bind off 10 sts, K to end (9 sts each side).

Left front: P 1 row. *Work St st for 3 rows.

Inc for front: Inc 1 st at neck edge (beg of K rows and end of P rows) on next 19 rows, marking side edge of the 15th row for armhole (28 sts). Work even in St st for 4 rows. Bind off*.

Right front: With wrong side facing, rejoin yarn to 9 right front sts, P to end.
Work as left front from * to *, but inc for neck at end of K rows and beg of P rows.

Rib band: With right sides facing, pick up and K52 sts from lower right front edge, around the neck edge, to lower left front. Work K1, P1 rib for 2 rows. Bind off.

Sleeves

Make two.
With right sides facing, pick up and K28 sts between armhole markers.
Work 10 rows in St st.

Next row: K2tog, K to last 2 sts, K2tog (26 sts).
Cont even in St st for 9 more rows.
Work K1, P1 rib for 2 rows. Bind off.

Ties

Make two. Cast on 28 sts. Bind off.

FINISHING

Sew the side and sleeve seams. Attach one end of each tie to the lower edge of each front.

To make the sweatband, measure around the doll's head and cut a piece of old T-shirt fabric to that length x 2" (5 cm), plus ¼" (6 mm) all around for seam allowances. Fold the band in half lengthwise, wrong sides facing, and sew the raw edges together, leaving an opening. Turn the band right side out and stitch the opening closed.

Extra Babe Things

Everything shown here can be made from bits of fabrics and embellishments scavenged from old garments, or yarn leftover from larger projects. Even the zipper on the ballet bag was rescued from a child's worn-out coat and cut down to size.

For this ballet skirt, cut a piece of floaty fabric on the bias to measure 32 x 7" (81 x 18 cm). Sew the short edges together, allowing a ¼" (6 mm) seam.

Make a casing (*see* page 25) for the elastic. Cut a piece of elastic to fit the doll's waist, thread it through the casing, and sew or tie the ends together. Sew a velvet ribbon around the waist for a feminine tie.

Fold over a double hem at the bottom and sew in place.

Add a felt flower, using the motif for the ballet bag on page 121.

For pas glissé or pas de chat, knit these miniature ballet slippers in girly pink yarn.

Make two. Beg at the toe end of the upper. With size 2 (2.75 mm) needles, cast on 3 sts. Work in St st, and K1f&b in the first and last stitch of every K row until there are 11 sts. Continue in St st for 3 more rows. (K2tog) twice, K3, (K2tog) twice (7 sts). Bind off.

For the soles, cast on 15 sts. Work St st for 4 rows. Cont in St st, K2tog in the center of every K row until there are 11 sts, ending with a P row. (K2tog) twice, K3, (K2tog) twice (7 sts). Bind off.

To make the ties, cut six lengths of yarn, measuring 16" (40 cm) each. Braid or twist three lengths together for each tie. Tie a knot to secure each end.

Sew the uppers to the soles, matching the cast-on end of the upper to the narrow end of the sole. Sew the center point of one tie to the center back of each slipper.

These simple sweats are made with fabric cut from an old T-shirt.

You will need a piece of T-shirt fabric measuring 15¾ x 11" (40 x 28 cm), and a length of ¼" (6 mm) elastic. Enlarge the pattern templates on page 111 to 167 percent. Cut out two pieces for each template.

Matching the fronts and backs, sew ¼" (6 mm) seams along the inside and outside legs. Turn one leg right side out and slip it inside the other. With right sides facing, sew the front and back gusset seams. Turn right side out.

Turn over a ⅜" (1 cm) casing around the waist edge. Stitch it in place, leaving an opening for the elastic. Cut the elastic to fit the waist. Thread the elastic through the casing and join the ends securely. Sew the opening closed.

Little fingers will adore this tiny felt ballet case with its zipper, handles, and flower motif!

Enlarge the ballet case templates on page 114 to 200 percent, and cut the shapes out of felt. Following the motifs on page 121, cut flowers out of different colors of felt.

With embroidery thread, sew the flowers to the felt circle for the front of the bag, adding a bead for decoration, if you wish.

Cut a slit in the edging strip and sew a zipper in place. Sew the band to the front and back circles, catching in the handles at the top, and positioning the zipper at the center of the top. With the zipper open, sew up the short seam at the base of the bag. Fill the bag with babe essentials, then zip it up.

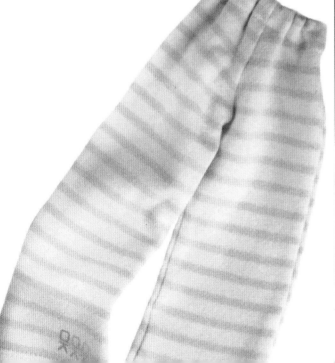

Rudy Ranch

Western wild 'n' free is red-haired, freckle-faced Rudy. This golden girl from the Big Country is as sweet as a summer sunrise. A rodeo rider and country girl with a fondness for fringed fashion, Rudy enjoys the great expanse and freedom of the open plains. She bunks down in a modest log cabin decorated in gingham and patchwork quilts, and spends her time riding and grooming her pony, Ranger.

Get-up
Yahoo Hat, Shirt, Vest, and Bell-bottoms • Ranch Skirt • Cowgirl Boots • Rodeo Hat • Rosette Tank • Cow Pants • Cozy Sleeping Bag • Cowgirl Print Denims • Saddle Picnic Basket • Floral Ho-Down Gown • Lacy Woolen Shawl

Yahoo Get-up

Everything Rudy needs for riding the open range

MATERIALS Fat quarter of checked fabric for shirt • Bias binding to contrast with shirt fabric • Scrap of retro fabric for pants • Scraps of felt for hat and star • ¼" (6 mm) elastic • Basic sewing kit • Sewing machine with zigzag stitch

NOTE All seams are ¼" (6 mm) wide and stitched with right sides facing, unless stated otherwise.

HAT INSTRUCTIONS

1 Photocopy or transfer the template on page 113 and cut the shapes from felt.
2 Zigzag the back seam of the crown side. Starting at the back seam, carefully zigzag the brim to the crown side, easing pieces to fit. Zigzag the brim back seam. Sew the crown top in place by hand.

CHECK SHIRT INSTRUCTIONS

1 Photocopy or transfer the template on page 118.
2 Fold checked fabric in half and pin the pattern pieces to it. Cut out the pieces and transfer the markings to the fabric.
3 Turn under and sew a ⅛" (3 mm) hem along the opening edges of both front pieces. Fold both pieces along the fold lines. Press the hems and folds.

4 Sew fronts to the back along the shoulder seams and press.
5 Sew the collar pieces together along the straight edges. Trim the corners and turn right side out. Press under the raw edges. Slip-stitch the collar to the neck edge of the shirt. Top stitch, close to the outer edges of the collar.
6 For the sleeves, sew the underarm seams. Press. Cut bias binding to fit around the bottom edge of the sleeves, adding seam allowances. Sew the two short ends of the binding together. Press in half lengthwise and top stitch the two folded edges to the sleeve. Turn back the cuff. Sew the sleeves into the armholes, matching the seams.
7 Fold under a double ⅛" (3 mm) hem around the bottom edge of the blouse and sew in place. Press.

VEST INSTRUCTIONS

1 Photocopy or transfer the template on page 112. Cut the shapes as directed.
2 Zigzag the back, shoulder, and side seams. Zigzag along both front edges for decoration.
3 Cut a ⅛" (3 mm) fringe along the bottom edge. Zigzag the pocket in place, leaving the top edge open.

BELL-BOTTOMS INSTRUCTIONS

1 Enlarge the templates on page 111 to
   167 percent. Cut out the pants, following
   the pattern for three-quarter length pants.

2 Sew each front to a corresponding back,
   along both the side and inside leg
   seams. Turn one pant leg right side out
   and slip it inside the other leg, right sides
   facing. Sew the front and back seams.

3 Make a ⅜" (1 cm) casing around the waist
   edge, leaving an opening for the elastic.

Thread elastic through the casing, tie or
sew it to secure, and sew the opening.

4 Turn under and sew a ⅛" (3 mm) hem
   around the bottom edge of each leg.

5 Cut two lengths of felt measuring 9 x 3"
   (23 x 7.5 cm) each for the leg fringe.
   Snip ⅛" (3 mm) cuts along each fringe
   strip. Sew the strips around the bottom
   hem of each leg.

6 Transfer the star motif on page 121 to a
   piece of felt. Zigzag the star on one leg.

Ranch Skirt, Cowgirl Boots, and Rodeo Hat

Calamity Jane rides again in gingham and felt

MATERIALS

32 x 7" (81 x 18 cm) gingham • Scraps of felt for horse motif, skirt fringe, boots, and hat • Four pearly beads • One small wooden bead • ¼" (6 mm) elastic • Basic sewing kit • Yarn for hat tie • Sewing machine with zigzag stitch

NOTE All seams are ¼" (6 mm) wide and stitched with right sides facing, unless stated otherwise.

RANCH SKIRT INSTRUCTIONS

1 Fold the gingham in half widthwise and sew the back seam.

2 Sew a ⅜" (1 cm) casing around the waist edge (for details, *see* page 25), leaving an opening for the elastic. Thread elastic through the casing, tie or sew to secure, and sew the casing opening closed.

3 Turn under and sew a ⅛" (3 mm) hem around lower skirt edge. Cut a length of felt to match the hem circumference. Snip ⅛" (3 mm) fringes along one long edge and sew to bottom edge of skirt.

4 Transfer the horse motif on page 120 to felt. Sew the motif to the skirt with a running stitch.

BOOTS INSTRUCTIONS

1 Photocopy the template on page 113 at 100 percent. Cut the shapes out of felt.

2 Place the boot fronts on top of the backs with wrong sizes together and zigzag the front seam to the toes.

3 Handsew a running stitch along the sole and around to the back of the heel.

4 Cut buttonholes on the outside of each boot. Sew two beads on each boot to match the holes. Snip fringes along the back of each boot.

HAT INSTRUCTIONS

1 Follow the hat instructions on page 98. Add a felt rosette, using the motif on page 120.

2 For the ties, cut four 12" (30 cm) lengths of yarn. Tape two lengths for each tie to a table. Twist the yarn until it is tight. Hold the ends firmly with one hand and hold the midpoint with the other hand. Take the loose ends to the taped ends and let go of the middle so that the yarn twists against itself into a cord.

3 Knot and trim the ends. Attach one end of each tie to each side of the hat. Thread loose ends through a bead and tie a knot.

Rosette Tank and Cow Pants

A fitted sleeveless rodeo top and cow-print pants

MATERIALS Fingering-weight cotton yarn in cream, red, white, and black • Size 2 (2.75 mm) needles • Tapestry needle • One pearly bead • Hook and eye • Shirring elastic for the pants

GAUGE 30 sts x 38 rows = 4" (10 cm) in St st on size 2 (2.75 mm) needles

TANK INSTRUCTIONS

Work the back and front alike.
Using cream, cast on 28 sts.
Work seed st as follows:
Row 1: *K1, P1; rep from * to end.
Row 2: *P1, K1; rep from * to end.
Rep last 2 rows once more.
Work in St st for 12 rows.
Shape armholes: K3, K2tog, K to last 5 sts, K2tog, K3 (26 sts).
Next row: P.
Rep last 2 rows until there are 14 sts.
Work 4 more rows in seed st. Bind off.

FINISHING

Sew the side seams and the right shoulder seam. Attach the hook and eye to each side of the left shoulder seam.

ROSETTE INSTRUCTIONS

Using red, cast on 57 sts. P 1 row.
Next row: K2, *K1, slip this st back onto the left needle, pass the next 8 sts over the top of this st and off the needle, yo twice, K the first st again, K2. Rep from * to end.
Next row: P1, *P2tog, P into the front of the first yo, then into the back of the second yo, P1; rep from * to last st, P1.
Next row: K2tog to end.
P 1 row.
Cut yarn, thread tail on a tapestry needle, draw it through the remaining stitches and pull to tighten. Fasten off. Sew it to the left shoulder, adding a bead in the center.

PANTS INSTRUCTIONS

Work the back and front alike.
Using size 2 (2.75 mm) needles and white, cast on 6 sts.
Row 1: K.
Inc row: P1f&b, P to last 2 sts, P1f&b, P1 (8 sts).
Rep the last 2 rows until there are 26 sts. At the same time, beg with the 13th row, work Rows 1–12 of the charted pattern from page 125. Work 4 rows even in St st. Bind off.

FINISHING

Sew the gusset and side seams, leaving openings for the legs. Thread shirring elastic around the top edge, pull to fit the doll's waist, and secure.

Extra Babe Things

This cozy sleeping bag can be made for any of the dolls, but it's an essential part of Rudy's western lifestyle.

You will need a piece of fabric measuring 15 x 14" (38 x 36 cm) each for the outer bag, the inner bag, and a similar piece of lightweight batting. You will also need two short lengths of fabric tape.

Lay the batting on a flat surface and place the two fabrics on top of it, right sides together. Sew the three layers together around all four sides, but leave a 3" (7.5 cm) opening along one short side for turning. Turn the piece right side out and sew the opening closed.

Fold the bag in half lengthwise with the outer fabric facing outward. Sew across the bottom edge and three-quarters of the way up the side. Attach a short length of tape on each side of the opening to make a tie.

Keep a lookout for the ideal fabric to fit your doll's character—like this denim "cowgirl" fabric for Rudy.

This denim print was just right for a pair of rough-riding rugged denims for Rudy. To make the pants, follow the instructions for Dot's Board Cords on page 38.

Of course, you could always use fabric from a worn-out pair of jeans. Choose the best bits of fabric and cut out the jeans using the templates on page 111. Be sure to include the small pockets or some of the stitching or studs for authentic details.

Make baskets and bags out of small scraps of yarn and fabric.

Make back and front alike.

Using size 2 (2.75 mm) needles cast on 21 sts.

Row 1: (K1, P1) 4 times, P5, (P1, K1) 4 times.

Row 2: (P1, K1) 4 times, K5, (K1, P1) 4 times.

Rows 3–7: Repeat Rows 1 and 2 twice, then work Row 1 once more.

Row 8: K7, (P1, K1) 4 times, K6.

Row 9: P7, (K1, P1) 4 times, P6.

Repeat last 2 rows twice, then work Row 8 once more.

Next row: (Work 7 sts in patt, mark position for handles) twice, work to end in patt. Bind off.

To make up: Sew front to back along sides and bottom. Cut flower motifs from felt and sew to bag, adding a bead if desired. For handles, thread a needle with 12" (30 cm) of yarn. Secure yarn to handle marker on one side of bag, make a loop, then secure to other handle marker. Loop the yarn back to the first marker, then work buttonhole stitches along the loop to cover it completely.

Make a casual floral dress by shortening the pattern for Bunny's Gingham Gala Gown.

Find a suitable print fabric and follow the instructions for Bunny's gown on page 54, shortening the skirt to 6" (15 cm). If you'd like, add buttonholes to make armholes.

Lacy Woolen Shawl

This handknitted shawl is full of country charm

MATERIALS Fingering-weight cotton yarn • Size 3 (3.25 mm) needles • Crochet hook

GAUGE 23 sts x 32 rows = 4" (10 cm) in St st on size 3 (3.25 mm) needles

INSTRUCTIONS

Cast on 34 sts.

Work in patt as follows:

Row 1: K1, *(yo, skp, K1) twice, yo, skp, (K2tog, yo, K1), twice, K2tog, yo; rep from * to last st, K1.

Row 2: P17, K1, P to end.

Row 3: *K1, (K1, yo, skp) twice, K2tog, yo twice, skp, K2tog, yo, K1, K2tog yo; rep from *, ending last rep yo, K2.

Rows 4 and 10: P9, K1, P15, K1, P to end.

Row 5: K3, *(yo, skp, K1) twice, K1, (K2tog, yo, K1) twice, K3; rep from *, ending last rep yo, K3.

Rows 6 and 8: P.

Row 7: K3 *(K1, yo, skp) twice, (K2tog, yo, K1) twice, K4; rep from *, ending last rep yo, K4.

Row 9: K5, *(yo, skp, K2tog, yo) twice, K8; rep from * to *, ending last rep K5.

Row 11: K1, (yo, skp, K3, yo, skp, K2, K2tog, yo, K3, K2tog, yo) twice, K1.

Rows 12 and 20: P17, K1, P to end.

Row 13: K1, (K2tog, yo twice, skp, K2, yo, skp, K2tog, yo, K2, K2tog, yo twice, skp) twice, K1.

Rows 14 and 18: (P3, K1, P11, K1) twice, P2.

Row 15: K1, (yo, skp, K2tog, yo) 8 times, K1.

Row 16: P5, (K1, P3) 7 times, P1.

Row 17: K1, (K2tog, yo twice, skp, K1, K2tog, yo, K2, yo, skp, K1, K2tog, yo twice, skp) twice, K1.

Row 19: K1, (yo, skp, K2, K2tog, yo, K4, yo, skp, K2, K2tog, yo) twice, K1.

Row 21: K1, (K3, K2tog, yo, K1, K2tog, yo twice, skp, K1, yo, skp, K3) twice, K1.

Row 22: P9, K1, P15, K1, P to end.

Row 23: K1, (K2, K2tog, yo, K1, K2tog, yo, K2, yo, skp, K1, yo, skp, K2) twice, K1.

Row 24: P.

Row 25: K1, (K1, K2tog, yo, K1, K2tog, yo, K4, yo, skp, K1, yo, skp, K1) twice, K1.

Row 26: P.

Row 27: K1, (K2tog, yo, K1, K2tog, yo, K1, K2tog, yo twice, skp, K1, yo, skp, K1, yo, skp) twice, K1.

Row 28: P9, K1, P15, K1, P to end.

Repeat Rows 1–28 twice more.

Bind off.

To finish: Add a fringe of seven or eight tassels across the top and bottom edges of the shawl. For each tassel, cut six 1½" (4 cm) lengths of yarn. Fold the bundle of six in half and use a crochet hook to pull the loop of the tassel through the knitting. Bring the loose ends of the tassel through the loop and pull to secure in place.

Dolly Bag

This drawstring bag, with its handy carrying straps, will keep your doll safe and clean, and leave plenty of room for her wardrobe. Make the bag before you start the doll, and use it to store your knitting and sewing.

MATERIALS Two pieces of patterned fabric for the main bag and lining, measuring 24 x 9" (62 x 23 cm) each • One 5½" (14 cm) diameter circle each of patterned fabric and lining fabric for the base • One piece of patterned fabric measuring 16 x 1¼" (41 x 3 cm) for the border • One piece of patterned fabric cut along the bias to measure 6 x 1¼" (41 x 3 cm) for the piping • One piece of piping cord measuring 16 x ¼" (41 x 0.6 cm) • 40" (1 m) cotton tape • Basic sewing kit • Safety pin

NOTE All seams are ⅜" (1 cm) wide and stitched with right sides facing, unless stated otherwise.

INSTRUCTIONS

1 Place the two pieces of patterned fabric for the main bag right sides together. Mark the position of the drawstring casing at two points on each long side, 1¾" (4.5 cm) and 2¼" (5.5 cm) from the top edge. Sew the seams on the long sides, leaving an opening between the markers. Turn right side out.

2 With right sides facing, sew the short ends of the border strip together. With wrong sides together, fold and press the border in half lengthwise. Press under ¼" (6 mm) along both long edges. Sew the border, catching both edges and aligning the seams, around the top edge of the main bag.

3 With right sides facing, sew the short ends of the bias strip together. Join the ends of the piping cord with a few stitches to form a loop. Fold the bias band in half lengthwise, wrong sides facing, and baste it in place over the cord.

4 Aligning the seams and raw edges, pin and baste the piping around the bottom edge of the main bag. Turn the bag inside out.

5 With right sides together, pin the patterned fabric base to the bottom edge of the main bag, clipping notches into the seam allowance as necessary to ease the fabric. Handsew it in place or machine sew using a zipper foot.

6 Make the lining as for the main bag, leaving an opening at the bottom of one seam for turning and omitting the piping. With right sides facing, fit the lining inside the bag, matching the side seams. Sew the lining to the main bag around the top edge.

7 Turn the bag right side out through the opening in the lining. Sew the opening closed.

8 Draw two parallel lines on each side of the bag to join the markers for the casing. Sew two rows of running stitches along the lines. Thread the tape through the casing, using a safety pin to guide it. Sew the raw ends together and secure them to the bottom of the bag.

Make the bag special by adding the doll's name in embroidered stitches. Add colorful designs and fancy stitches to complement the fabric of the bag.

Templates

The templates on the next few pages are used for the sewn garments and accessories. Follow the instructions given with the templates, and within the project pages.

Many of the templates are shown at the correct size. Others will need to be enlarged on a photocopier at the percentages given. Measurements are also given for the final width and length measurements so that you'll know at a glance how much fabric you'll need.

Photocopy the templates (to the correct enlargement if necessary) then use the photocopy as a pattern for cutting the fabric, or trace the pattern onto tissue or tracing paper first, if you prefer. The heavy, solid lines represent cutting lines, the dashed lines represent sewing lines, and dotted lines represent folds.

The patterns allow for ¼" (6 mm) seam allowances, unless stated otherwise. To ensure that the garment will hang properly, always align the arrow on the pattern with the straight grain of the fabric, either lengthwise or widthwise.

GOWN

For Bunny's Sparkly Ribbon-tied Gown, you'll need just the Bodice Front. For Bunny's Flower Power Mini, you'll need both the Bodice Front and Bodice Back.

Enlarge the pattern pieces to 143 percent.

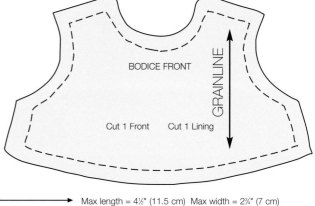

BODICE FRONT

GRAINLINE

Cut 1 Front   Cut 1 Lining

Max length = 4½" (11.5 cm) Max width = 2¾" (7 cm)

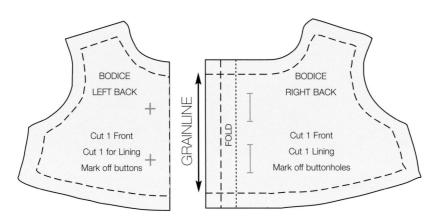

BODICE LEFT BACK

Cut 1 Front
Cut 1 for Lining
Mark off buttons

GRAINLINE

FOLD

BODICE RIGHT BACK

Cut 1 Front
Cut 1 Lining
Mark off buttonholes

PANTS AND SHORTS

Use this pattern at its full length for Dot's Board Cords and Flo's Stripy Sweatpants. Use the three-quarter length for Rudy's Yahoo Bell-bottoms, and for DD's Flamenco and Denim Bell-bottoms. Use the short length for DD's Rainbow Shorts.

Enlarge the pattern pieces to 167 percent.

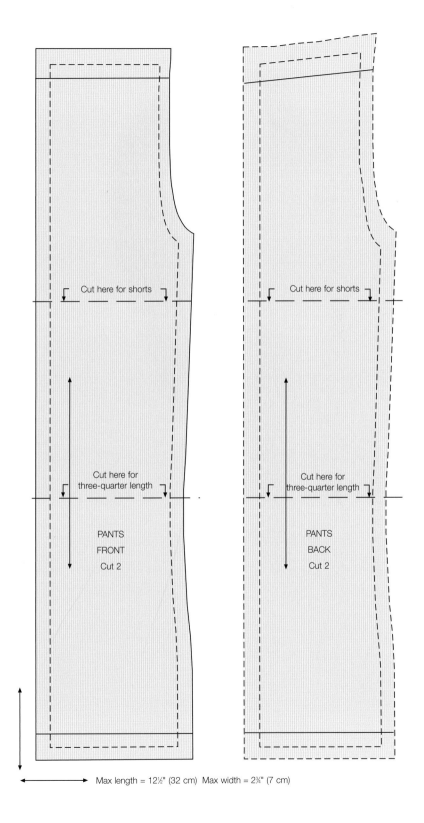

Cut here for shorts

Cut here for three-quarter length

PANTS
FRONT
Cut 2

Cut here for shorts

Cut here for three-quarter length

PANTS
BACK
Cut 2

Max length = 12½" (32 cm) Max width = 2¾" (7 cm)

VEST

There is no need for a seam allowance here—simply lay the edges next to each other and zigzag them together.

Use the pattern pieces at 100 percent.

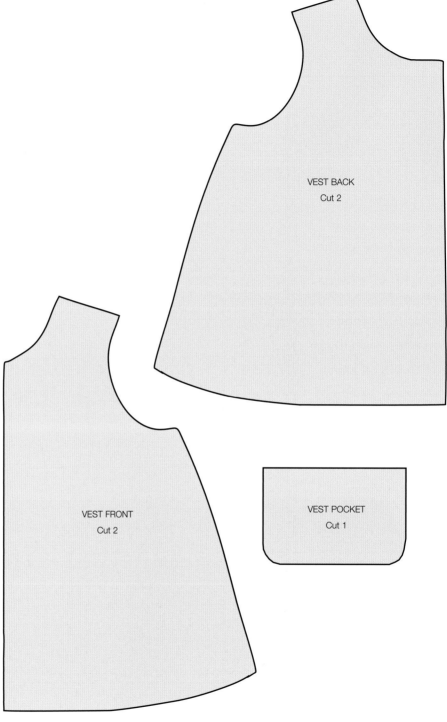

VEST BACK
Cut 2

VEST FRONT
Cut 2

VEST POCKET
Cut 1

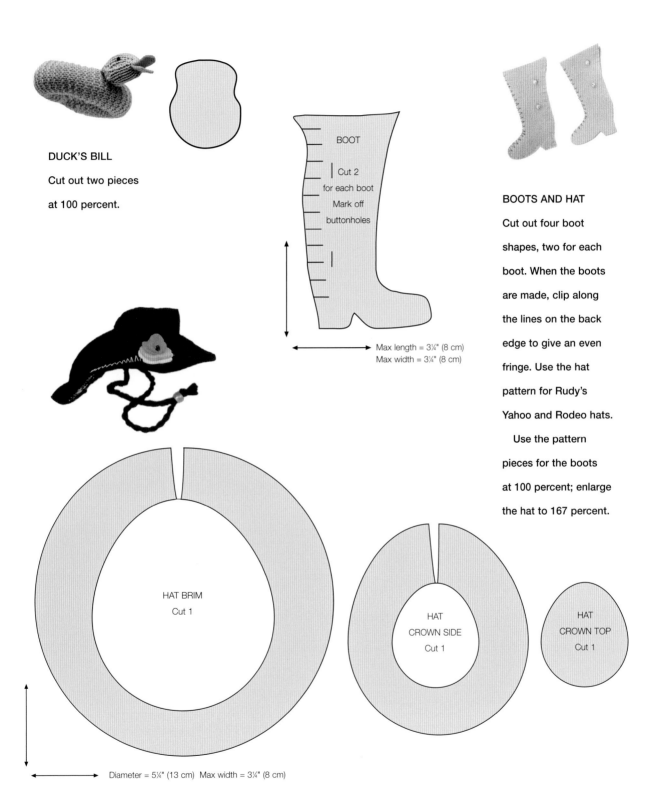

DUCK'S BILL

Cut out two pieces at 100 percent.

BOOT

Cut 2 for each boot Mark off buttonholes

Max length = 3¼" (8 cm)
Max width = 3¼" (8 cm)

BOOTS AND HAT

Cut out four boot shapes, two for each boot. When the boots are made, clip along the lines on the back edge to give an even fringe. Use the hat pattern for Rudy's Yahoo and Rodeo hats.

Use the pattern pieces for the boots at 100 percent; enlarge the hat to 167 percent.

HAT BRIM
Cut 1

HAT
CROWN SIDE
Cut 1

HAT
CROWN TOP
Cut 1

Diameter = 5¼" (13 cm) Max width = 3¼" (8 cm)

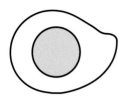

BALLET CASE HANDLE

Cut 2

BALLET CASE
FRONT & BACK
Cut 2
Diameter = 3" (7.5 cm)

BALLET CASE EDGING Length = 8¼" (21 cm) Width = 1" (2.5 cm)

Zipper length = 4¼" (11 cm) Width = 1" (2.5 cm)

EYE AND LIPS

Use the eyes and lips
at 100 percent, or
enlarge or reduce them
as you desire.
Follow the dashed line
on the lips to stitch it
to the doll.

BALLET CASE

Enlarge the pattern
pieces to 200 percent.

50s BAG

Embellish the bag with
a faux emerald bead.

Use the pattern
pieces at 100 percent.

50s BAG
FRONT & BACK
Cut 2
Mark off bead position on one side

X

FOLD

50s BAG
FELT FLAP
Cut 1
Cut slit for fastener

50s BAG STRAP   Cut 1

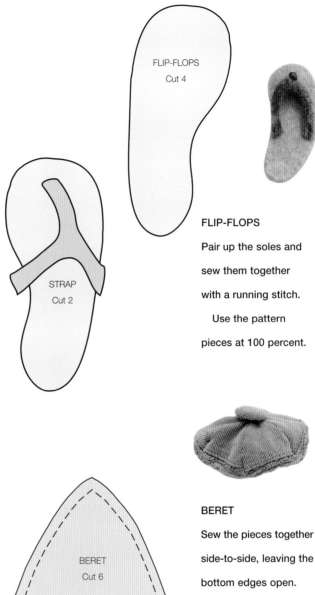

SEQUIN BAG STRAP   Cut 1

SEQUIN BAG

Cut out the template
and fold the felt along
the dotted lines as you
would an envelope.

Use the pattern
pieces at 100 percent.

FLIP-FLOPS

FLIP-FLOPS
Cut 4

STRAP
Cut 2

FLIP-FLOPS

Pair up the soles and
sew them together
with a running stitch.

Use the pattern
pieces at 100 percent.

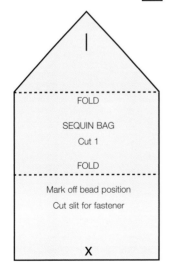

I

FOLD

SEQUIN BAG

Cut 1

FOLD

Mark off bead position

Cut slit for fastener

X

BERET
Cut 6

BERET

Sew the pieces together
side-to-side, leaving the
bottom edges open.
Attach a button to the
top.

Enlarge the pattern
pieces to 143 percent.

DRESS

You'll need two fabrics for Bunny's Psychedelic A-line—one for the dress and another for the lining.

Enlarge the pattern pieces to 143 percent.

DRESS
LINING FRONT
Cut 1

GRAINLINE

DRESS
FRONT
Cut 1

GRAINLINE

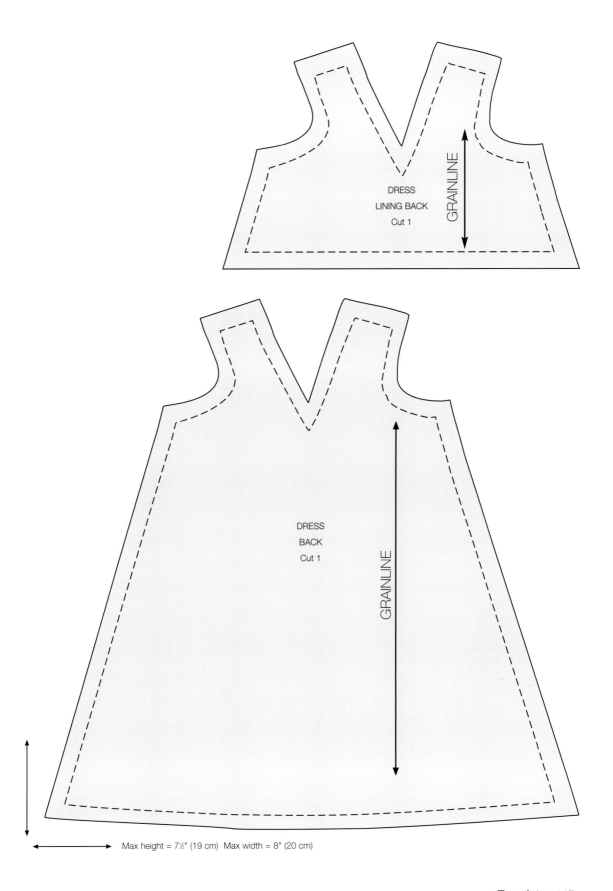

DRESS
LINING BACK
Cut 1

GRAINLINE

DRESS

BACK

Cut 1

GRAINLINE

Max height = 7½" (19 cm) Max width = 8" (20 cm)

BLOUSE AND SHIRT

Use this pattern without the Collar Stand, for Rudy's Yahoo Shirt.

Use this pattern without the Sleeve, for Dot's Sleeveless Seersucker Blouse.

Use the pattern pieces at 100 percent.

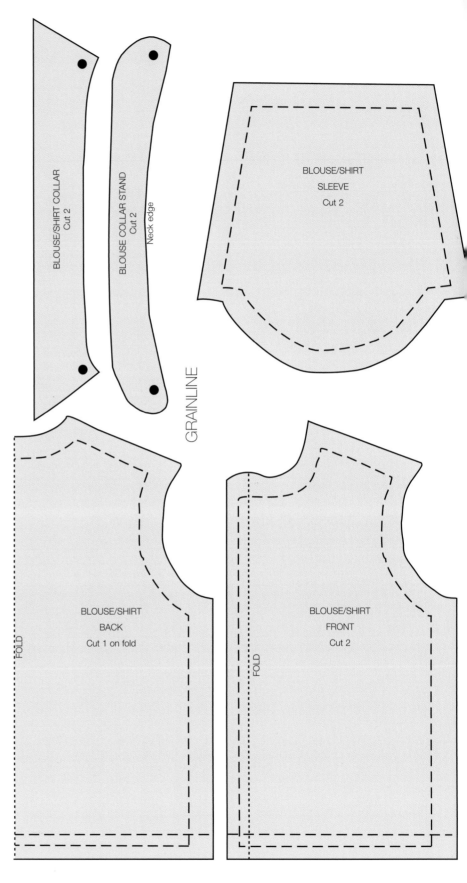

BLOUSE/SHIRT COLLAR
Cut 2

BLOUSE COLLAR STAND
Cut 2

Neck edge

BLOUSE/SHIRT
SLEEVE
Cut 2

GRAINLINE

FOLD

BLOUSE/SHIRT
BACK
Cut 1 on fold

FOLD

BLOUSE/SHIRT
FRONT
Cut 2

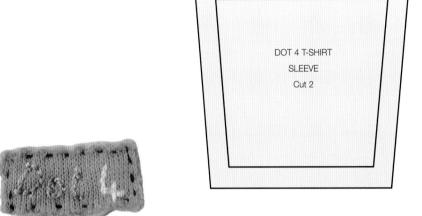

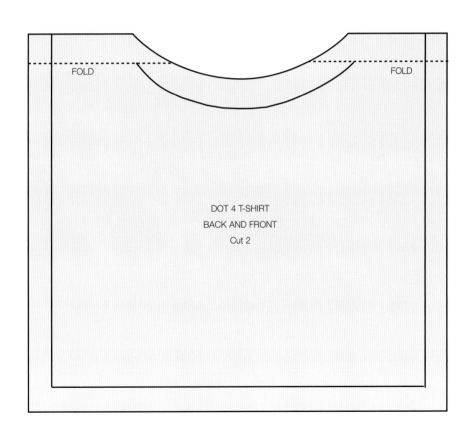

DOT 4 T-SHIRT

To get a totally patchwork effect, sew together small pieces of several fabrics, then cut the pattern pieces out of the patchwork fabric. A scrap of knit fabric with hand embroidery adds to the charm.

Use the pattern pieces at 100 percent.

DOT 4 T-SHIRT
SLEEVE
Cut 2

FOLD

FOLD

DOT 4 T-SHIRT
BACK AND FRONT
Cut 2

Motifs

Whether for Dot's Board Cords or DD's Go Paradise Travel Bag, scraps of felt can provide the finishing details for all of babe's essentials.

Use the motifs shown here to bestow a touch of femininity, cheeky charm, or humor to the garments and accessories. Add even more gorgeous or glitzy detail by combining different colors of felt, working some embroidery stitches, or attaching fabulous beads. Be adventurous and create more motifs of your own design.

Use the motifs at 100 percent. Note that some of the motifs combine layers of different shapes, each one in a different color. Use felt for these tiny adornments— it comes in a wide assorment of colors, is easy to work with, and will not ravel.

Be sure to attach the motifs securely to the garment or accessory. Usually a single sturdy stitch or an outline of running stitches is sufficient.

For Bunny's Butterfly Slippers, work two long stitches along the center of the butterfly shape to define the body. Attach flowers and stars with a single stitch in the center, or embellish the stitch with a decorative bead, as for Flo's Ballet Case or Rudy's Rodeo Hat.

Attach the horse and saddle to Rudy's Ranch Skirt with running stitches. Also use running stitches to sew the plane to DD's Go Paradise Travel Bag. Add longer stitches to detail the cockpit and the wording on the label before attaching them.

paradise

Knitting Charts

The charts on the following pages are for the color patterns used in some of the knitted garments.

Each square represents one stitch; each row of squares represents one row of stitches. The striped squares represent ribbing. Odd-numbered (knit) rows are numbered on the right and even-numbered (purl) rows are numbered on on the left. Read the charts from right to left for knit rows, and from left to right for purl rows. Always read the charts from bottom to top.

FAIR ISLE PULLOVER

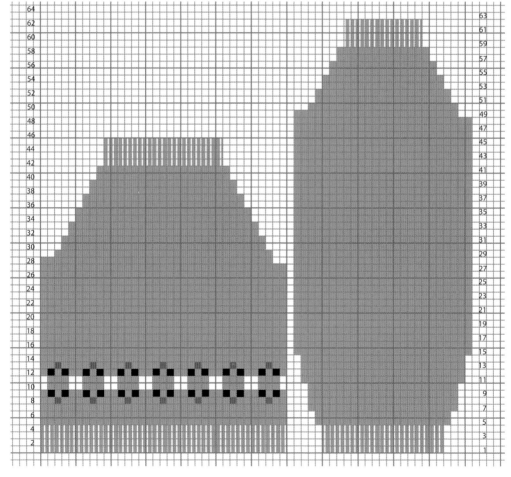

FRONT AND BACK Knit 2

SLEEVE Knit 2

FRONT

BACK

LIFESAVER BATHER

When you reach row 23, begin working the lifesaver ring motif. Start the white yarn at the beginning of the row, stranding it across the back and catching it on every third stitch. Knit 13 sts in red, introduce the white and knit 2 sts, then drop the white and knit another 13 sts in red.

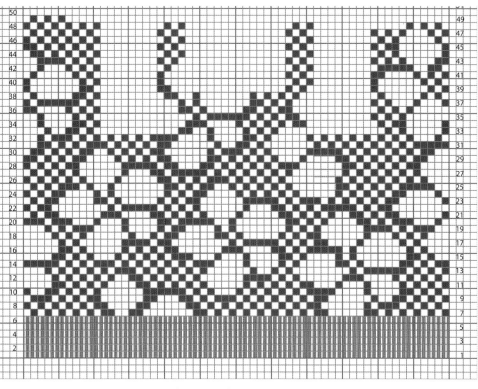

RETRO PINK POLO

Begin with the rib, then

work the floral pattern

by stranding the

unused yarn across

the back of the work.

FRONT AND BACK Knitted in 1 piece

BLUE BUBBLES

CARDIGAN

The bubble pattern is

only worked on the left

sleeve and right front.

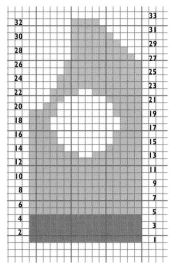

RIGHT FRONT

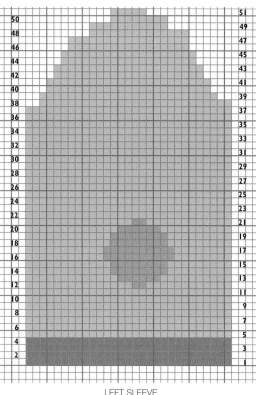

LEFT SLEEVE

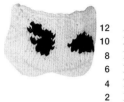

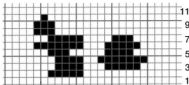

FRONT AND BACK

COW PANTS

Begin the color pattern

on Row 13 of the pants.

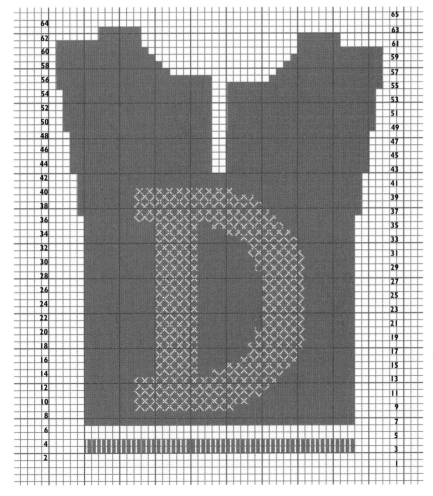

FRONT

D HOODY

Work the "D" motif only on the hoody front, beginning on Row 9 as follows: Knit to the point where the motif starts, purl 14 sts for the first row of the "D", then knit the rest of the row. On the next row, purl as usual, but knit the stitches of the "D" motif. Continue in this way to "reverse out" the "D" until the motif is complete.

KEY

knit on RS rows
purl on WS rows

purl on RS rows
knit on WS rows

Babes' Care

Taking care of your special creation is as important as making it.

You'll find immense joy in making the loveable babes and their wardrobes from discarded clothing and scraps of leftover yarns and fabrics. Not only will you make something out of "nothing," you'll also have the opportunity to bring life to memories associated with old treasures such as your child's first dress or your favorite cashmere. If you decide to use new fabrics, be sure to wash them ahead of time to avoid unexpected shrinkage later.

To keep your work clean until it is complete, store it in a clean bag or pillowcase. Or use the Dolly Bag on page 108 to protect your babe-in-progress. When your babe is completed, she'll feel right at home in the bag!

Most of the sewn garments can be washed in a machine on a normal warm-water cycle. However, those garments that contain special finishes, such as beads or sequins, should be carefully washed by hand.

Refer to the yarn bands to identify special washing instructions for the knitted pieces. Many of today's wool and cotton yarns can be machine washed on a delicate cycle. Most any yarn can be washed by hand. After washing and rinsing, reshape the damp garment, if necessary, then lay it flat away from direct heat or sunlight, and let it air-dry completely.

Index

Acknowledgments

I would like to thank Anna, Tim, Christine, and Catherine at Mitchell Beazley, as well as Karen and Marilyn—you are all brilliant. Also my mother, Wendy, for helping with the knitting of the seemingly endless arms, legs, and bodies.

Babes, similar to the ones featured in this book, are available as a knit kit—visit www.dotpebbles.com; and for suppliers of yarns similar to those used in the book visit www.knitrowan.com.